POPULAR MANUFACTURING MYTHS

Eliminating Widely Held Beliefs That Reduce Competitiveness

DOUGLAS B. RELYEA

POPULAR MANUFACTURING MYTHS

Eliminating Widely Held Beliefs That Reduce Competitiveness

CRC Press
Taylor & Francis Group
Boca Raton London New York

CRC Press is an imprint of the
Taylor & Francis Group, an **informa** business

A PRODUCTIVITY PRESS BOOK

MIX
Paper from
responsible sources
FSC® C014174

CRC Press
Taylor & Francis Group
6000 Broken Sound Parkway NW, Suite 300
Boca Raton, FL 33487-2742

© 2013 by Taylor & Francis Group, LLC
CRC Press is an imprint of Taylor & Francis Group, an Informa business

No claim to original U.S. Government works

Printed on acid-free paper
Version Date: 20121207

International Standard Book Number: 978-1-4665-6660-6 (Hardback)

Library of Congress Cataloging-in-Publication Data

Relyea, Douglas B.
   Popular manufacturing myths : eliminating widely held beliefs that reduce competitiveness / Douglas B. Relyea.
      pages cm
      Includes bibliographical references and index.
      ISBN 978-1-4665-6660-6 (alk. paper)
      1. Manufacturing processes. 2. Competition. 3. Profit. I. Title.

TS183.R445 2013
658.5--dc23   2012043735

Visit the Taylor & Francis Web site at
http://www.taylorandfrancis.com

and the CRC Press Web site at
http://www.crcpress.com

Contents

Preface

While reading *The Growth of American Thought* (Merle Curti, Harper, New York, 1943), I was intrigued by an unfamiliar word. Mr. Curti, addressing the period in American History that dealt with the Great Depression, described as *shibboleths* the many current theories regarding the root cause of the economic state of the country.

Dictionary.com offered several definitions for the word *shibboleth*, but the definition that caught my attention was

> shib-bo-leth (shib-uh-lith): a common saying or belief with little *current* meaning or truth.

I then went to the definition of *belief* and was rewarded with the following:

> be-lief (bih-leef): confidence in the truth or existence of something not immediately susceptible to rigorous proof, a statement unworthy of belief.

Several weeks later while visiting a new client company, I had the opportunity to participate in a meeting of manufacturing and research and development engineers for the purpose of discussing several specific and expensive problems related to an injection molding process.

The discussion was dominated by ideas, proposed solutions, and suggested causes of product problems typically preceded by qualifying statements, such as "we believe," "I think," "we are sure," and the like. One question pertaining to the raw material was addressed with a statement that the raw material in question was always accompanied by a certificate of conformance (C of C) provided by the supplier. After a brief discussion, the group realized that none of the data on any of the C of Cs received by the company over the years had ever been internally qualified as accurate.

The shibboleth, the myth, the opinion, in this case, was the common belief the C of Cs always provided an accurate description of certain raw material parameters critical to the customer's process. No proof of the accuracy of C-of-C data was ever asked for or provided, and after an appropriate investigation, it turned out the C of Cs did not reflect the quality of the product they accompanied.

That evening, I came across another shibboleth while reading *A World Undone, the Story of the Great War* (G.J. Meyer, Random House, New York, 2006). The horrors of World War I trench warfare were well known at the time, yet the civilian populations of the British/French/Russian alliance (the Entente) were purposely misled into thinking their side was on the brink of victory while suffering far fewer casualties than the enemy.

> The Entente propagandists depicted almost every fight in the West as a slaughter of Germans mounting robotlike suicide attacks, when in fact, German losses were often markedly lower than those of the Entente. Back in London, the army's director of military operations produced an analysis supposedly demonstrating that Germany was going to run out of men "a few months hence."

I found this shibboleth especially interesting because it is a classic example of how a baseless belief not only can be created but also individuals very likely close to the originators—the army's director of military operations in this case—begin to believe and propagate the shibboleth themselves.

Many years ago, I became shibboleth-centric without realizing it because for a long time I have constantly asked for some basis of proof, some data source that will substantiate a belief, a myth, or an opinion that had become part of a local manufacturing culture.

Myths, paradigms, shibboleths, and shop floor tribal knowledge, all variations on the same theme, are widespread in manufacturing and, almost without exception, serve to limit competitiveness. Throughout this book, I use these terms interchangeably.

I find myths to be part of the culture within specific departments of manufacturing and service companies. I find opinions to be part of the culture of entire companies. I find shibboleths part of the culture of communities large and small. I hear shibboleths on the news, in political statements, in commercials, and so on.

I have never encountered a shibboleth, myth, or opinion that was not, in some way, counterproductive, and I have come to realize shibboleths exist because many people are reluctant to ask for some proof that will support a statement of "fact."

In the following chapters, I hope to demonstrate why people need to begin asking for proof when presented with widely held popular beliefs, whether those beliefs are related to a business decision or our personal life.

This is why I wrote *Popular Manufacturing Myths: Eliminating Widely Held Beliefs That Reduce Competitiveness.*

1

Introduction to Manufacturing Myths

The danger of speaking out and the danger of remaining silent balance agonizingly in our minds.

George Clemenceau

My purpose in writing *Popular Manufacturing Myths* is not to paint a negative image of manufacturing practices but rather to raise an awareness that deeply rooted counterproductive convictions exist, to varying degrees, throughout manufacturing and service industries. Having a conviction related to a manufacturing process is not, in itself, counterproductive except when the conviction is not supported by data.

On average, I participate in over one hundred meetings a year for the purpose of discussing manufacturing process problems, acquisition of new equipment, customer complaints, raw material defects, and so on. Statements made by participants in these meetings are most often front ended with "In my opinion ... ," "I believe ... ," or some other qualifier that implies that the speaker's offering is not based on or supported by any form of data or data-related facts. Quite the contrary, by definition, an opinion or belief is devoid of facts.

Opinion and *belief* are respectively defined as "resting on grounds insufficient to produce complete certainty" and "the existence of something not immediately susceptible to rigorous proof." By their very definitions, beliefs and opinions are not based on data and, like myths, legends, shibboleths, and the like have no place in responsible decision making related to manufacturing processes.

The subtitle of this book, *Eliminating Widely Held Beliefs That Reduce Competitiveness,* is perhaps a slightly more accurate description of the purpose of this book. In this book, I attempt to provide an insight into some of the more common manufacturing myths regularly encountered in the manufacturing environments that negatively influence competitiveness. I also suggest reasons why the myths exist as well as possible remedies that might be applied to dispel specific myths. I classify the various myths into *management myths, shop floor myths,* and if appropriate, *shared management and shop floor myths.* Finally, when possible, I offer case studies with a few specifics changed to protect the "guilty."

Making decisions based on data is a discipline. As such, there are certain rules that apply to collecting and structuring the data so that it is meaningful and instructive. To this end, I have taken great pains to present the basics of data collection tools, techniques, and analysis, and I suggest simplistic methods of structuring the data to assist in communicating logical conclusions. However, and this is important, I have not cluttered up my explanations with high-browed statistical theories or give instruction on how to perform expensive and intrusive process studies.

I am sensitive to two real facts of manufacturing life:

- Providing tools that interfere with production does not enhance a company's competitiveness.
- Not everyone is a statistician, and not everyone wants to be.

I have written this book keeping in mind my "prime directive": do not interfere with the production process.

I have tried desperately not to exceed the most basic of arithmetic concepts of averaging and the basic statistical concept of normal variation and the histogram.

However, for those who wish to know a little bit more of a statistical concept to which I allude, I provide Chapter 8, "Addendum." This chapter offers brief explanations and, in some cases, sample calculations for those who wish to understand a little bit more about a particular concept, technique, tool, or procedure.

Data collection tools and data-based problem-solving techniques that interfere with normal manufacturing processes have no place on the shop floor.

Nor am I am suggesting that all opinions or beliefs related to manufacturing are wrong, but before they are applied to expensive decisions, an effort should be made to verify them with data. This is a simple concept that is not always easily accomplished.

THE HUMAN FACTOR

Opinions that are not well founded on data typically exist because of someone's past experience. As a result, a person's opinions become extremely personal. Many people "own" their process opinions, fiercely defend the veracity of their process opinions, and see no need to confirm their process opinions with data.

Challenge a person's opinion about a process, and you are, in essence, challenging the person; that typically results in conflict, increased resistance to new data collection ideas, and impasse. To quote Thomas Jefferson: "I never saw an instance of one of two disputants convincing the other by argument."

A frontal attack on a widely held, deeply ingrained opinion, belief, myth, or shibboleth is, more often than not, doomed to failure. On the other hand, a simple data-based event that does not interfere with the manufacturing output can help people decide for themselves whether a specific element of tribal knowledge is valid.

Data is impartial to opinions. For instance, two manufacturing myths that are virtually universal in industry are also closely related and extremely difficult to dispel. These two myths are as follows:

SHOP FLOOR MYTH

I can make frequent, small adjustments to the equipment in order to keep everything I produce exactly on target.

MANAGEMENT MYTH

A machine operator is not doing his or her job if he or she is not constantly making small adjustments in order to make as much product as possible at the target value.

NATURAL VARIATION

With respect to these two manufacturing myths, I cannot imagine which came first, but experience dictates that each one seems to feed on the other. And, both exist because there is a fundamental lack of understanding in many organizations of the basic concept of natural variation, sometimes referred to as normal variation.

When broaching the topic of normal variation with manufacturing managers and associates, I lead off by asking them if they can get to work every day in exactly the same amount of time—down to the second. Of course, the answer is "no." Everyone accepts the idea that normal traffic patterns and daily changes in the weather alone will introduce variation into the time it takes an individual to get to work each day.

If we accurately monitored the amount of time it took someone to get to work every day for three months and placed the data into a histogram—literally a picture of history—we would likely develop a graphic such as in Figure 1.1. Figure 1.1 is a classic example of normal variation, natural variation, or as it is sometimes referred to for obvious reasons, the bell-shaped curve. No matter what you prefer to call this phenomenon, it is part of everyday life as well as manufacturing processes.

In the briefest of terms, this person arrives at work, on the average, sixteen minutes after leaving the house. When traffic is heavy and weather is foul, it will take this individual twenty minutes to get to work; conversely, when fair weather prevails and traffic is light, he will arrive at work twelve minutes after leaving home.

The normal curve is the extent of statistical concepts that will be discussed in this book.

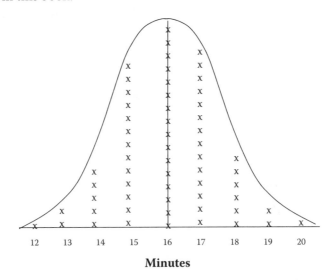

Minutes

FIGURE 1.1
Histogram of daily time to work.

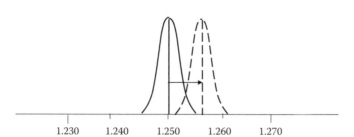

FIGURE 1.2
The effect of operator adjustments on diameter.

In spite of the fact that we are surrounded by examples of normal variation in our daily lives, the very existence of normal variation seems to be largely ignored in manufacturing. The majority of machine operators believe they can optimize the product they have been charged to produce by constantly measuring and adjusting operator-controllable process parameters such as tensions, temperatures, pressures, and the like. Figure 1.2 illustrates the effect of operator process adjustments on a product characteristic such as diameter.

The following three case studies demonstrate several facets of what I believe to be a very common manufacturing myth that is generally shared jointly by shop floor and management personnel.

MANAGEMENT AND SHOP FLOOR SHARED MYTH

The effect of normal variation ceases to exist at the entrance to the manufacturing shop floor.

In the first case study please make note of the difficulty in getting a cross section of managers, supervisors and operators to allow a process to produce product for any length of time without making adjustments.

In the second case study the reader will note the laudable desire on the part of the pressman to make 'perfect product' which, by itself, speaks to the lack of recognition of normal variation.

And finally in the third case study the standard setup procedures, which are created for the purpose of reducing the operator component of normal variation, were totally disregarded—due to a lack of understanding—resulting in the near loss of a critical customer.

WALL THICKNESS CASE STUDY

A manufacturer of specialty electronic wire and cable was having a great deal of difficulty in maintaining the appropriate wall thickness of the insulated material being extruded onto copper conductor. The thickness of the insulated material—referred to as the wall thickness—was specified by the customer to be 0.045 ± 0.0025 inches (0.0425 to 0.0475 inches). The problem was that quality audits of the insulated wire indicated the wall thickness was ranging from under the low specification of 0.0425 inches to over the high specification of 0.0475 inches. This was a problem because multiples of the insulated wire were eventually combined to form a cable approximately two inches in diameter. The cable was designed to be pulled through preformed holes in the airframe of commercial aircraft under construction.

Obviously, if the wall thickness of any one individual wire was under the low customer specification, it might cause a serious electrical malfunction after installation, not a desirable event at 30,000 feet. On the other hand, if a number of wires over the high wall thickness were cabled together, the overall diameter of the cable might be subjected to abrasion by the airframe during or after construction, which could also cause a serious electrical malfunction.

Supervisors and operators were constantly reminded of the absolute necessity to keep the wall thickness within the customer specification. Yet, in spite of all the online inspections performed by the operators, quality audits consistently found reels of extruded wire that had undersize and oversize wall thickness.

A meeting was held with a group consisting of an engineer, a manufacturing technician, and several quality inspectors, all of whom had been working on this problem for several months. During the meeting, shop floor practices were discussed, and some historical wire diameter data, recorded by the operators, was reviewed. A second meeting was scheduled, but this meeting was to include two extruder operators responsible for producing the single end wires that were demonstrating the out-of-specification wall thickness.

At the next meeting, the operators were understandably frustrated. They explained that they used a machinist microscope to measure the wall thickness of the insulation; one measurement was taken and recorded at the end of each reel produced. However, no matter how often they measured the wire and no matter how many adjustments they made to maintain the diameter at the nominal, the quality auditors regularly found product wall thickness outside specification. The concept of normal variation was discussed as well as the example of normal variation as it relates to coming to work every day. The operators were familiarized with the fact that their extrusion process would also evidence normal variation in the wall thickness of extruded wire.

All product characteristics have a certain degree of variation due to the variation of equipment, raw material, people, and methods. It would be unnatural for an operator to measure a critical characteristic over a period of time and *not* have different results (see Figure 1.3).

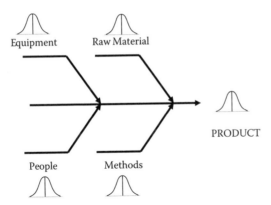

FIGURE 1.3
Process variation causes product variation.

It is a common belief, especially among equipment operators, that a process output can be maintained exactly at a desired target—usually the customer's nominal—by taking numerous measurements and making small adjustments in the (false) belief that they are resetting a drifting process to their desired target. As a result of this false belief, operators collect data more often to make more adjustments to maintain the product characteristic more often at the desired target.

To a lesser degree, experience has demonstrated that some members of management believe an operator who is not making constant adjustments is not doing the job of maintaining the critical product characteristics at the target.

Generally, the only method of overcoming these deeply ingrained beliefs is to convince everyone involved to allow the process to produce product for a period of time without making adjustments, periodically record measurements, and plot the measurements on a histogram or control, which is nothing more than a histogram turned on its side. This concept is discussed further in Chapter 4.

The suggestion was offered to have one operator, after she had determined the process was producing quality product, allow the process to operate for an entire shift without making any adjustments. The only other difference was that she was asked to reduce the length of each reel by 50 percent to allow a minimum of twenty end-of-reel measurements by the end of her shift. She was requested to select a sample, as usual, at the end of each reel and measure and record the wall thickness; the supervisor and coordinator of the study were standing by if she had any concerns or questions.

The operator, Susan, was very uneasy about allowing the process to run without making adjustments; she was concerned that she would be held accountable for making defective product. The supervisor, also suspect of this procedure, was not effective in convincing Susan as he was concerned that the production manager would fault him for allowing Susan to stand idly by while the process produced excessive scrap. Finally, after a meeting that included the general manager, the production manager, the supervisor, the shop steward, Susan, and me, all parties—some reluctantly—agreed to the plan to allow the process to run for an entire shift without operator adjustments. The only caveat was as follows: If three consecutive measurements were either ascending or descending, it would be prudent to make an adjustment but to note the time and the nature of the adjustment.

Susan established the process in her usual manner, which did not necessarily agree with the way her colleagues on the other shifts established the same process, a topic discussed in a subsequent chapter. As usual, Susan made adjustments and measured wall thickness until she was satisfied the process was producing product to the appropriate wall thickness customer nominal of 0.045 inch. At this point, Susan was reminded to refrain from making any adjustments to correct for wall thickness differences in subsequent measurements.

At the end of the first reel, Susan measured the wall thickness as 0.0435 inch, and she instinctively began to make an adjustment but was gently reminded to allow the process to demonstrate what it was capable of achieving without constant adjustments. At one point during her shift, Susan had two consecutive ascending wall thickness measurements, and she insisted the process was drifting out of control. Once again, it was necessary to assure her that she would not be held responsible if product was made above the high specification.

At the end of her shift, the data Susan collected, representing twenty-seven reels, was put into a histogram, and the results were shared with everyone involved.

A histogram—literally a picture of history—is one of the simplest, most effective manufacturing analysis tools because it requires no arithmetic, and it can provide a simple graphic of a process output.

It is apparent from Figure 1.4 that the wall thickness variation, in the absence of compensatory adjustments, was quite capable of producing the product well within the customer's specification.

It became apparent that the operators had been so sensitized to the need to maintain the wall thickness within specification that they were attempting, by continuously making adjustments to the process, to produce everything exactly at nominal. And, contrary to what everyone believed, by making constant adjustments to the process parameters, the operators were causing wall thickness to change.

Consider that at the end of a certain reel the process is centered exactly at the customer's nominal value of 0.045" (see curve A of Figure 1.5). But, due to random variation, the sample measured by the operator just happened to measure 0.0445—perfectly normal and well within specification. However, prior to the understanding created by introduction to the histogram, the operator would be inclined to make an adjustment to "bring the wall thickness up to nominal." The result of this unnecessary adjustment is illustrated in Figure 1.5, curve B.

In this wall thickness case study, the operators, supervisors, and other members of management were laboring under the unsubstantiated

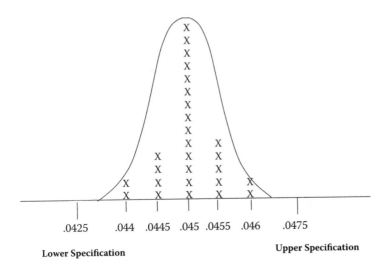

FIGURE 1.4
Susan's data representing twenty-seven consecutive wall thickness measurements.

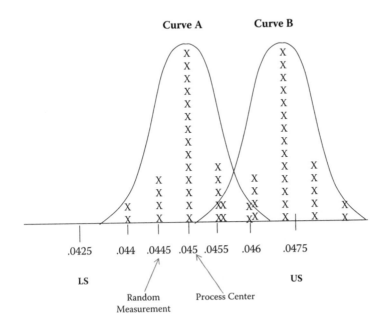

FIGURE 1.5
Histogram as a result of adjustments.

belief/myth that an adjustment was prudent any time a measured sample was not exactly at nominal. They had never been introduced to the concept of normal variation as it applies to manufacturing processes and, with the best of intent, had been creating serious process shifts by constantly over-adjusting based on a single random sample taken at the end of each reel.

This one brief study, which in no way interfered with normal flow of production, did not serve to thoroughly convince everyone on the shop floor that it was not necessary to constantly "tweak" process parameters to maintain control of wall thickness, tensile, elongation, outer diameter, and so on.

Machine operators, regardless of the industry, take a great deal of pride in the belief that they can produce (with their particular technique, setup, and pattern of adjustments) better product than their colleagues operating the same equipment on different shifts.

In this case, the very personal shop floor myth that *I can make frequent, small adjustments to the equipment in order to keep everything I produce exactly on target,* and I can do it better than anyone else, was being attacked. In short, the operator's sense of craftsmanship was threatened.

It took months of training in the basic concepts of normal variation, and repeating Susan's experiment over and over, before the operators, and certain managers, began to accept as invalid the widely held opinion/belief/myth/shibboleth regarding the need for constant adjustments.

Of course, it took time for a number of supervisors and other members of management to deal with their own deeply ingrained myth that *a machine operator is not doing his or her job if he or she is not constantly making small adjustments in order to make as much product as possible at the target value.* One supervisor was even heard exclaiming "If they're not making adjustments all the time, what exactly *will* they be doing?"

It is amazing what equipment operators can accomplish if they are not constantly monitoring product characteristics and compensating for perceived changes in the product by making adjustments to the process.

Depending on the type of process and company culture, operators, rather than constantly measuring and making adjustments, could spend their time

- Staging and preparing raw material
- Checking quality of material coming from an internal supplier
- Organizing tools
- Cleaning equipment
- Performing some preventive maintenance
- Performing internal audits on standard procedures
- Running a second piece of equipment
- Policing the area
- Reading and understanding equipment manuals

AN ADJUSTMENT IS AN ADJUSTMENT

For over twenty-five years, I have visited manufacturing facilities ranging from the Canadian province of Saskatchewan to the Caribbean island of Hispaniola and many points in between. I have presented public seminars that hosted manufacturing professionals from Saudi Arabia to Costa Rica. In all my travels and all my contacts with people attending my seminars, I have discovered the one common factor that exists universally throughout manufacturing is that shop floor associates firmly believe continually adjusting processes is correct, proper, and necessary.

IS IT OK IF I TWEAK?

I had the opportunity to work with a company that manufactures printed material for U.S. corporations by employing state-of-the-art offset and gravure printing technology. At one time in my relationship with this organization, I had occasion to coordinate a study similar to the wall thickness case study. In this instance, the concern was color density, which is a critical metric that serves to determine the quality and consistency of the printed image.

I met with the first shift pressman at the beginning of his shift and explained in detail that our plan was to determine how much color density variation was normal for this particular press, and to accomplish this, we would need him to set up the press as usual and, once he was satisfied with his color density measurements, allow the press to run without making further adjustments for color density. He was also requested to make note of any changes to the equipment, such as introducing a new batch of ink, changing a plate, and so on. Finally, if during his shift he felt the need to make an adjustment to color density because the product became visually unacceptable, he should feel free to make the requisite changes to maintain product quality but also to make note of the adjustment. Once again, the goal is always to learn about the process without interfering with the normal flow of production.

I met with the other two pressmen at the beginning of second and third shift to ensure each pressman received, understood, and agreed to help us achieve our collective goal.

The pressmen and their assistants and helpers were extremely cooperative; a great deal was learned about the capability of the process, especially the equipment. Of course, the results of the study were shared with the shift supervisors, pressmen, and other participants.

The most interesting aspect of this particular study was a conversation I had with one of the pressmen. To better understand the significance of this exchange, it is necessary to point out these pressmen normally have in excess of twenty years of experience in offset printing technology, and they consider themselves to be part pressman, part mechanic, part pressroom engineer, part artist, and part magician and, in some cases, rightly so.

The subject pressman of this anecdote listened politely to and agreed to my requests. The only comment he had came in the form of a question:

> If a particular color is visually almost perfect and the density reading is well within specification, can I "tweak" it a bit? Not much, mind you, just a bit to make it perfect. That's not to be considered an adjustment is it? I don't need to record that do I? I mean … I tweak the press all the time; this is why I put out better product than the other shifts.

When a manufacturing facility comes to realize that a key component of improved competitiveness is the standardization of shop floor manufacturing practices, it must also accept that standardization includes equipment operators setting up and running processes according to standard operating procedures (SOPs) without making adjustments, which includes tweaking. I am familiar with SOPs that do not allow for adjustments, and I have come across SOPs that allow for adjustments that must include a justification for the adjustment as a case for a permanent change to the SOP.

However, I have never seen an SOP that allows for indiscriminant adjustments or tweaking for the purpose of making good product better. And yet, indiscriminant adjustments being made by well-intentioned operators seem to be the order of the day in manufacturing, and in cases such as the offset pressman, some adjustments are not even considered to be adjustments.

CRIMPED CONNECTOR CASE STUDY

A U.S. automotive company contracted with an electronic component manufacturer to provide a ten-inch long, laminated flexible assembly designed to connect the automobile radio to the power, speakers, and ancillary equipment terminated in the dashboard. Four individual lead wires extending beyond the laminated portion of the assembly served to provide the necessary electrical connection to the bus bar in the dashboard.

The electrical connections were formed by mechanically crimping terminals from a large, narrow reel of terminals to the four lead wires; the narrow reel or "pancake" automatically fed the terminals into a die that the operator activated with a foot pedal to crimp the terminals to the leads. There were four separate crimping operations for each part.

The diameter of the finished crimped terminals was critical to provide a proper fit when mated to the dashboard bus bar. Almost from the very first shipment, the supplier received sales returns and complaints due to oversize and undersize terminal diameters. The oversize terminals would not easily fit into the precisely designed bus bar, which slowed production, and the undersize terminals fell out of the bus bar after point of sales, resulting in warranty claims.

Management's response to the initial customer complaints and returns was to have the die operators use handheld micrometers to measure the four crimp diameters on one finished part for every twenty-five assemblies. If an out-of-specification crimp was discovered, the die or the pneumatic pressure would be adjusted.

The returns and complaints continued.

The next corrective action was to have a sample of 125 assemblies selected from each lot of approximately 2,300 finished parts. The diameters of four terminals on each of the 125 assemblies were measured with a micrometer, and if any crimped diameters were out of specification, the entire lot was sorted 100%. Many parts were scrapped, and the remainder of the parts were shipped.

The returns and complaints continued.

The machine operator sample inspection was discontinued, and part-time high school students were hired to 100% inspect every finished crimped terminal. Rejects piled up at considerable cost.

The returns and complaints continued.

After several months of returns and complaints, I was invited to participate in helping to solve this problem the day after the automotive customer informed the supplier that continued rejects would result in the business being moved to a competitor.

A study similar to the wall thickness case study and the offset press color density study was suggested and accepted by management.

Meetings were conducted with all three shifts, and once again, instructions were given not to make any adjustments for a period spanning all three shifts.

Production ran smoothly for the next twenty-four hours; data was collected and laid out in three histograms to demonstrate the results to the operators and supervisors involved in the study. Figure 1.6 clearly demonstrates three different bell-shaped patterns representing the histograms, one for each shift. For illustration, this graphic is not exactly to scale. For a better understanding of the impact of the adjustments, please see Chapter 8, "Control Charts."

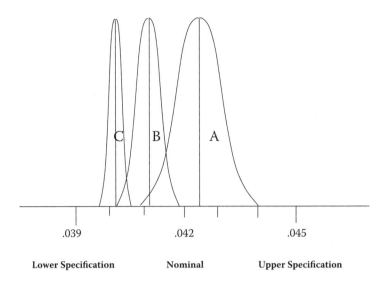

FIGURE 1.6
Shift-specific bell-shaped curves.

Please note that each bell-shaped curve has a different center, indicating process average shifts between shifts, and each of the three curves demonstrates a different width. Either the operators were making adjustments or there were erratic changes occurring in the equipment or raw material that were specific to each shift.

Meetings were conducted with the operators and supervisors, engineers, technicians, quality auditors, and others. Questions asked and respective answers included the following:

Were adjustments made between shifts?	No
Did raw material change between shifts?	No
Did the electrical load change between shifts?	No
Did ambient temperatures drastically change?	No
Were there equipment failures?	No

In desperation, it was decided to ask the second-shift operator, Lucinda, to explain to us everything she did from the moment her shift began at 4:00 p.m. until she left at 12:30 a.m.

Lucinda began by telling us she punched in and went to her locker to collect her box of tools, Magic Markers, and so on. Then, she had to search for "her" chair, which was always being used by other people on first shift, and of course, she had to adjust her table, calibrate her micrometer, and so on. After all the preliminaries were concluded sometime around 4:30 p.m., she reached up and loosened the knurled knob on the pancake spindle and rotated the pancake counterclockwise to take up the slack in the feed tape. Lucinda made an adjustment.

When reminded she was not supposed to make any adjustments to the process during the study, she insisted that what she did was not an adjustment, "it was part of her setup."

It turned out Lucinda and her colleague on third shift had adopted the same setup procedure and had modified the SOP to include keeping the slack tight on the feed. Of course, each lady had her own subjective idea regarding what a "tight" feed was—ergo the differences between the three shifts.

IN CONCLUSION

Constant or even frequent adjustments should not be part of a machine operator's daily regime. If constant or frequent adjustments are deemed necessary, something is wrong with the process or the operator is being overscrupulous in attempts to make everything meet a specific target. Either way, counterproductive myths are at work, and the manufacturing facility's competitiveness is being adversely affected.

In the following chapters, I discuss what I have found to be the source or root cause of the various five categories of manufacturing myths. I offer case studies as well as suggestions for discrediting each particular myth.

2

Expectational Myths

Anger always comes
from frustrated expectations.

Elliot Larson

Manufacturing myths, legends, shibboleths, and the like come about as a result of a purposeful intent on the part of a person or persons or they grow out of prevailing circumstances. However, regardless of how a myth is born or created, the one element common to all manufacturing myths is people. Not only must people be involved in the birth or creation of a myth or shibboleth, but also they contribute to its growth, maturation, and solidification as part of a company's culture.

I arrange manufacturing myths into two classes:

- Shop Floor Myths
- Management Myths

However, the reader will note that some myths such that found in Chapter 1. The Effects of Normal Variation Cease to Exist at the Entrance to the Manufacturing Shop Floor Myth are sometimes shared by the shop floor as well as management.

I further consider there are seven main categories of manufacturing myths. I specify main categories because at times a Myth such as the one referenced above results in a spin off. In the three Case Studies in Chapter 1 the spin off myth involved the perceived need to make constant adjustments to the process in question.

In this chapter I will address:

- Expectational Myths

In subsequent chapters I will discuss the following categories of Myths.

- Chapter 3: Data Myths
- Chapter 4: Our Process Is Different Myth
- Chapter 5: Measurement Process Myths.
- Chapter 6: Only One Adjust One Process Parameter at a Time Myth
- Chapter 7: Raw Material Myths
- Chapter 8: Addendum
- Chapter 8 Individuals Chart Detection Rules
  - One data point falling outside either three sigma limit.
  - Two of three consecutive data points falling outside either two sigma limit.
  - Five consecutive data points falling on the same side of the centerline with one of the data point falling outside either one sigma limit.
  - Six consecutive data points falling on the same side of the centerline.

In the first seven chapters, I strive to avoid algebraic formulas and statistical theories when discussing why some myths exist and ways to perhaps dispel them. I have not engaged in mathematics and statistics because I would prefer the average manager and shop floor associate be able to read the first seven chapters and understand the essence of discussion without the statistical mumbo jumbo that frustrates many interested readers of books related to improving manufacturing competitiveness.

Chapter 8 provides a reference to those readers who would like a brief explanation of those concepts discussed in the previous seven chapters that are based on statistical theories and mathematics.

For the balance of this chapter, I offer an insight into several other expectational myths.

EXPECTATIONAL MYTHS

Once again, all levels of an organization have certain expectational myths that are, in all probability, due to value imprinting resulting from past experiences and associations. Once an expectational myth or shibboleth is born, it is nurtured and spreads throughout a manufacturing facility by input passed on from senior shop floor associates to newcomers. It can even be introduced from the outside by a recently hired employee who was "infected" with the myth as a result of association with a former company. And, an expectational myth or shibboleth, like most false perceptions that have no basis, can become as if etched in stone and, as such, not easily dispelled. Some expectational myths also have a penchant for contributing to the creation of other baseless perceptions.

Two Safety-Related Expectational Myths

SHOP FLOOR MYTH

Management places production concerns above safety.

MANAGEMENT MYTH

Every accident is thoroughly investigated, and the root cause of the accident is identified and corrected.

Safety versus Productivity

The unfortunate and most-often-wrong shop floor impression that management cares about productivity above safety is due to the following simple facts:

- Any successful management group reviews data related to production efficiencies, quality, safety, scrap rates, and the like on a shift-by-shift basis and responds to any problems reflected by the data.
- Shift data most often indicates problems in the areas of low efficiencies, poor quality, absenteeism, and high scrap, which, of course, receives immediate management attention and thus has high visibility on the shop floor.
- Fortunately, shift data rarely indicates that an accident occurred; therefore, safety would not *regularly* receive the same high visibility on the shop floor as the other management concerns.
- Management's interest in safety-related matters other than accident investigations is normally addressed in meetings scheduled for the purposes of investigating acquisition of ergonomic equipment, planning for safety seminars, qualifying safe raw materials, and so on.

Minutes of such meetings are often published and posted, but such minutes certainly do not have high visibility on the shop floor.

- The lack of high visibility on the shop floor of management's conference room safety activity results in the shop floor myth that management cares less about safety than other shop floor issues.

I have never known a management group that was not equally or more concerned about safety as about productivity issues. But, at risk of repetition, the most visible aspect of management's concern regarding safety only rises to the surface in the rare event of an accident. And, because accidents fortunately do not happen on every shift of every day, it may very well appear to the casual observer that management is not as concerned about safety as about productivity.

Accident Reports

There is one tangible contribution to the myth that management places more emphasis on productivity than on safety. This contribution comes from the typical accident investigation report, usually completed by a departmental supervisor.

All too often the accident investigation becomes cursory. Too many reports identify the cause of the accident to be "operator inattention" and the corrective action recorded as "informed the operator to pay more attention." In many manufacturing facilities, there is seldom an adequate root cause analysis performed to determine the actual cause of the accident.

> **ACCIDENT REPORT CASE STUDY**
>
> I once read an accident report that described how a lady had cut her hand while grabbing for a round-handled X-Acto knife that had rolled off her trim station workbench. The report listed the cause of the accident as "the operator reflexively grabbed for her X-Acto knife as it rolled off the trim station workbench." The corrective action was recorded as "told the operator not to reflexively grab for her X-Acto knife if it is rolling off her workstation."
>
> It took about 5 minutes to revisit the accident, identify the root cause, and submit a work order to fabricate a small rim around the workstation to keep things from rolling off.

Root cause analyses are seldom performed correctly when investigating accidents.

Remedy

Management can contribute to dispelling both of the safety-related myths:

SHOP FLOOR MYTH

Management places production concerns above every other aspect of our business.

and

MANAGEMENT MYTH

Every accident is thoroughly investigated, and the root cause of the accident is identified and corrected.

The elimination of both myths would be advanced by providing simple problem-solving education to those individuals who investigate the accidents as well as those members of upper management who give final approval and sign off on all accident reports.

At the very least, investigators of accidents need to involve the person who suffered the accident, as well as bystanders, and the question "Why?" needs to be asked five times.

"Why did Carol cut her hand?"
"She grabbed for the knife as it was falling to the floor."
"Why was the knife falling to the floor?"
"Because the knife handle is round, and the bench is not perfectly level."
"Why is the bench not level?"
"Because the floor is not level."
"Can we easily level the floor?"
"No."
"Then how can we keep the knives from rolling off the benches?"
"We can put molding around the edges of the benches."
"Thank you."

Identifying the root cause of problems is often not difficult, but it takes some education, and that is, of course, a management responsibility.

Quality-Related Expectational Myth

SHOP FLOOR MYTH

Management cares about quality only when it does not conflict with *production efficiencies.*

Productivity versus Quality

The myth that management cares about quality only when it is convenient stems from at least three culturally acceptable practices that have been adopted by some companies.

- Dual specifications
- Internal deviations
- The quarantine override

In many manufacturing organizations, written policies often address the importance of maintaining quality. "We strive to exceed our customers' quality expectations" is a popular phrase. Shop floor associates read these policies and often determine the flowery words do not balance with their perceptions of in-house attitudes and practices of management.

An example of this apparent imbalance between what is written about in policy statements and more than likely discussed at companywide meetings is found in what appears to the shop floor as management's inconsistent attitude toward quality when product is found to be out of specification.

Dual Specifications

One cause of this apparent inconsistency can often be the result of a management decision to have two sets of specifications for certain product characteristics. One specification is represented by the customer-supplied nominal dimension plus and minus a tolerance band. The other specification is an "internal" requirement represented by management's decision not only to maintain the customer-supplied nominal but also, in an effort to ensure out-of-specification material does not slip by the operator, to tighten up or narrow the customer-supplied tolerance.

For example, consider the customer's specification for a critical shaft diameter to be 0.500 plus or minus 0.010 inch. This would translate to lower and upper specifications of 0.490 and 0.510 inch, respectively.

When an internal specification is developed by management, it is customary to narrow the customer specification by adding an arbitrary value to the lower specification and subtracting the same value from the upper specification. In this case, we will assume management has added 0.002 inch to the lower specification and subtracted 0.002 inch from the upper specification. This narrowed internal specification of nominal plus and minus management's new tolerance provides the internal shop floor specification of 0.500 plus or minus 0.008 inch or 0.492 to 0.508 inch.

Please understand that with this internal specification the operator believes it is his or her responsibility to manufacture the critical shaft diameter between 0.492 and 0.508 inch. This in spite of the fact the customer specification is 0.490 to 0.510 inch (see Figure 2.1).

This concept of dual specifications—one for the customer and one for the shop floor—is often applied to a critical product characteristic or to a characteristic that has been, in the past, problematic. And, for reasons I have never been able to fathom, some management groups believe that creating a narrower specification for the shop floor will somehow prevent the operator from manufacturing parts that are out of the customer's specification.

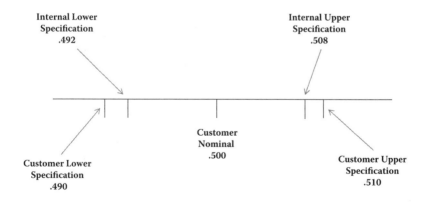

FIGURE 2.1
Internal specifications.

As a matter of fact, contrary to what some managers might think, the dual-specification practice can contribute to an attitude that will cause out-of-specification product to be manufactured and shipped.

Consider that at some point in time a conscientious operator performing periodic quality checks on the product he or she is manufacturing might very well find the diameter in question to be under his or her low specification of 0.492 inch or above his or her upper specification of 0.508 inch.

Assume, for discussion purposes, the operator records a measurement of 0.5095 inch; this is a measurement 0.0015 inch above what is the permissible upper specification according to the work instruction. When the operator brings this to the attention of the shift supervisor, who is aware of the true customer specification, the supervisor, of course, authorizes the operator to continue producing product.

When the supervisor says, based on knowledge of the customer's true requirements for this critical specification, "That's OK; they'll take it, keep running," the supervisor is sending a signal to the operator that a little bit out of specification is acceptable. In essence, he or she is communicating the impression that being a little bit out of specification does not justify stopping production. Keeping the line going is more important than shipping product that is a little bit out of specification to the customer.

As a practical matter, what else can the supervisor say? He or she is management's representative on the shop floor, knows the customer specification is 0.490 to 0.510 inch, but cannot share that with the operator because he or she would be undermining the very reason, invalid as it may be, behind management's decision to have two sets of specifications.

I risk repetition when I, again, state that I do not understand why a management group would establish the practice of maintaining two sets of specifications. What is the benefit of giving the shop floor one guideline knowing that a minor violation will be accepted by the supervisor?

This practice of setting a dual specification is wrong on a number of levels: It causes frustration for the operators, undermines the credibility of the supervisor, and gives rise to the myth that management promotes quality only when quality does not interfere with productivity.

Consider that a history of supervisors allowing "out-of-specification material" to leave the department without taking steps to sort out the defective material and shutting down the process to adjust tooling or otherwise correct the process will, as stated, eventually result in operator frustration. Think how frustrating it would be to follow the work instruction, report what is certainly a deviation from that work instruction, only to be told repeatedly that the identified problem is not really a problem.

Perhaps most damaging of all, this myth can cause serious quality problems at the customer location.

At some point, the operator frustration will result in the slightly out-of-specification conditions not being reported to the supervisor at all; instead, the operator will just keep producing product. Why would any reasonable and prudent person bother reporting every time there is a 0.001 to 0.002-inch violation of either upper or lower specification only to be told this condition will be accepted by the customer?

It would seem reasonable to remove the "middleman" and just keep on making product when the operator discovers product slightly out of specification.

And, if the customer will accept product that is outside the shop floor specification by as much as 0.0015 inch, the customer will probably accept product that is 0.002 inch outside the shop floor specification. These situations have a way of getting out of hand, and at some point in time operators may decide that parts with diameters 0.0025 inch outside of specification are "OK."

As a matter of fact, a new operator who has been informed by his or her shop floor mentor that 0.0025 inch outside of specification is OK may decide that if 0.0025 inch is OK, the occasional part at 0.0035 inch outside of specification would also be acceptable to the customer.

Of course, 0.0035 inch outside the internal specification is, in fact, only 0.0015 inch outside the true customer specification.

And, the occasional diameter that is 0.0015 inch outside the customer specification will not necessarily wreak immediate havoc at the customer location.

It needs to be recognized that because an operator finds the occasional random part 0.0035 inch outside the internal specification (0.0015 inch outside of customer specification), it does not mean the entire product being produced by that operator, on that machine, at that time is 0.0015 inch out of the true specification.

The shaded area of Figure 2.2 represents the estimate of the percentage of parts over the customer upper specification by 0.0015 inch.

There will always be a certain amount of normal variation about the average diameter of the parts being manufactured.

If the average diameter of the product being manufactured is somewhat higher or lower than the customer nominal, only a very small fraction of

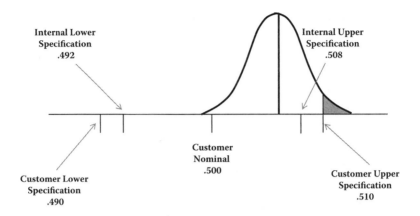

FIGURE 2.2
A significant shift may result in only a small percentage of out of specification product.

what is being produced will be as much as 0.0015 inch outside the customer specification. The vast majority of what is being produced is more than likely within the actual customer's specification.

This is not to say the customer should be happy with even the smallest amount of out-of-specification product, but as a practical matter, it could be some time before the customer discovers any of the small percentage of product produced, in this scenario, as much as 0.0015 inch outside the true specification.

It will only be a matter of time before the customer sends back a shipment with tagged samples that measure as high as 0.5115 inch, a full 0.0015 inch above their upper specification of 0.510 inch.

In one instance with which I was involved, the operator explained that, "Yes, on occasion a single random sample would measure 0.0035 inch over specification," but she had ceased to report to the supervisor when she was running up to 0.002 inch over specification. At one point, she had measured a random sample to be 0.0035 inch over the upper specification, but the supervisor was in a meeting. She knew that management did not want the line shut down. She had passed diameters in the past that were as much as 0.0025 inch over specification and was not aware of any customer rejects, so she decided that if the customer would accept parts with diameters 0.0025 inch over specification, "they would probably use parts with diameters 0.0035 inch over specification."

This is often the result of a tight specification when it is loosely enforced.

Internal Deviations

Some manufacturers include customer specifications in the shop floor work instructions and address out-of-specification product through a formal system of internal deviations. This practice requires the operator to inform the supervisor of out-of-specification material, at which time the supervisor is required to fill out and submit a standard form to the engineering department or the sales department that, in essence, is a request to continue producing and authorizing the shipment of product that does not meet the customer specification.

The basis for such a formalized system is the belief that the engineer, based on his or her knowledge of the end use, can determine if the out-of-specification characteristic will cause a problem for the customer. The sales department is often included in this procedure based on the assumption that it is familiar with how sensitive the customer might be to this particular aberration.

Some organizations even have a material review board (MRB) that periodically convenes to review shop floor deviation requests. Some MRBs are populated with individuals from production, sales, research and development (R&D), and engineering and one member of upper management.

Many requests for deviation are hand walked through the required series of signatures by the supervisor because of the need to maintain production and shipping schedules. And, of course, approved deviations are maintained on file. This is necessary in order to provide a defense if and when parts are returned by the customer for being out of specification or, God forbid, legal action follows a field failure involving an assembly that contained the out-of-specification part.

Naturally, the shop floor associates are very familiar with such deviation processes, and it would be equally as natural for them to conclude that management will "strive to exceed" the customer's quality expectations when it is convenient and cost effective and does not interfere with production or shipping schedules.

The bureaucracy of internal deviation processes is very transparent to the shop floor, and it is another reason the manufacturing associates are led to believe management places productivity ahead of quality. I have found that, in the majority of instances, when internal deviations have become a part of doing business, it is the result of a "wink and a nod" between supplier and customer. Both parties recognize the specification in question was applied rather arbitrarily, and a certain product characteristic some-what above or below the specification will, in fact, work quite well in the application for which it was designed.

The creation of "arbitrary specifications" is discussed further in this chapter.

Rather than change the specification, there is tacit agreement that product slightly out of spec will be processed at the customer's facility, ergo the internal deviation process at the supplier facility. Of course, the customer's facility more than likely has an incoming raw material deviation process in the event *its* operators notice out-of-specification product.

More than once, I have heard the plaintive cry from the shop floor, "Why don't they just change the specification?"

I asked the same question many years ago while working for a company that supplied the automotive industry. I was told it cost several thousand dollars for an automotive manufacturer to change one blue-print specification.

This was a reasonable answer, but I wondered at the time if anyone had ever evaluated the cost of the deviation bureaucracies at supplier and end-user facilities. The monetary cost, I suspect, would be substantial. The cost to management's reputation for quality would be even more of a concern.

The Quarantine Override

Finally, there is the phenomenon involving product that was deemed by members of management to be rejected product, tagged with the appro-priate red "rejected" stickers and placed in a quarantine area only to be reevaluated by a senior member of management, who discovers the product is, in fact, acceptable after all. I can offer no explanations or apolo-gies for a quarantine override other than for economic purposes a senior member of management is willing to take a chance on shipping borderline quality product.

This may not happen that often, although anecdotally I have seen it close to the end of the month in a slow period when anticipated billing for the month has come up short. However, it only has to happen once to rein-force the shop floor belief that management gives voice to the importance of quality but does not always abide by their policy statements.

Another expectational myth is closely related to the first in that it is founded on internal specifications that are often arbitrary.

The Sales and Marketing Connection

MANAGEMENT MYTH

The manufacturing facility is capable of meeting whatever specification the customer requires.

The myth that *management cares about quality only when it does not conflict with production efficiencies* would not exist if management established a very simple procedure for ensuring the output of the manufacturing processes met all the specification requirements before accepting a purchase order.

The same can be said of the myth about to be discussed.

It is imprudent to assume that because a customer wants to have a plus or minus 0.0025-inch tolerance on a critical characteristic that a particular process is capable of maintaining that characteristic within those customer-required bounds. This brings us to another expectational myth generally found alive and well in many sales and marketing departments.

I mean no disrespect to sales and marketing professionals all over the world, but they cannot *expect that the manufacturing facility is capable of meeting whatever specification the customer requires.* This may seem like a commonsense statement because no responsible sales or marketing professional would dream of accepting a purchase order he or she knew could not be properly serviced. But, unfortunately the typical sales or marketing professional is not necessarily aware of what the manufacturing processes back at the plant are capable of maintaining.

To carry my point one step further, in many manufacturing organizations even the people back at the plant do not *know* what the in-house processes are capable of achieving by way of maintaining a certain tolerance.

When I say they do not "know," I mean they cannot point to data that has been properly collected and analyzed therefore they cannot express in numerical terms, the capability of a process to produce to product that will meet the customer's specification.

The in-house staff may have a good idea of the capability of the process based on experience. After all, they have been making and shipping product for years, and the scrap, rework, and returns have been minimal. But, they do not *know*, based on simple arithmetic, how the variation of the critical characteristic compares to the customer specification.

As a matter of fact, the minimal scrap, rework, and returns experienced in the past could very well be due to the fact the natural variation of critical dimensions is exceeding the customer specification.

Now, I would like to add that most customer specifications are, at best, arbitrary. I offer this rationale based on two obvious facts:

- Customers establish specifications for product to be provided by a supplier company with very little to no understanding of the supplier's processes.
- It appears to be a universal practice that all blueprints and specification sheets created and issued by hundreds of companies indicate tolerances that are typically an even multiple of five or evenly divisible by five.

Specifically, the vast majority of blueprint specifications I have encountered over the years are plus and minus 0.001, 0.005, 0.002, 0.0005, 0.010 inch and so on. I have never seen a specification of plus and minus 0.0017 inch. The same phenomenon is true regardless of the metric. Elongation, tensile, pH levels, durometer, hardness, and so on generally always have specifications that are evenly divided by five. I refer to this phenomenon as the "multiple-of-five specification rule."

I think the multiple-of-five specification rule is due to the fact that God provided us with five fingers. Somewhere in this vast universe of ours, there may be a planet of six-fingered beings, and I expect their specifications will be subject to the multiple-of-six specification rule. That would be plus and minus 0.006, 0.012, 0.036, and so on.

Levity aside, the multiple-of-five specification phenomenon implies specifications are, as a rule, identified without benefit of any analyses that would result from selecting and measuring random samples and applying some simple arithmetic.

Perhaps some specifications are determined by running the process for an appreciable amount of time, measuring random samples, and setting the specification based on the highest and lowest measurement. Or, perhaps operators are interviewed, and their experience is used to set the high and low boundaries of a characteristic. Neither method would stand up to immediate rigorous proof demonstrating the origin of the specification.

In fact, a simple and inexpensive process capability study is the only acceptable method to determine the boundaries that should be applied to a characteristic. The execution of a process capability study is beyond the scope of this book; however, the several books listed in the bibliography are excellent resources that will provide an understanding of how to benefit from the simple process capability tool. Also, the reader may refer to the section in Chapter 8 on process capability studies.

DISPELLING THE MYTHS

The myth that *Management places production concerns above every other aspect of our business* stems from the lack of drilling down to the root cause of accidents as well as the root cause of production problems. Volumes have been written addressing how to identify the root cause of any problem, and it is beyond the scope of this work to go into the details. However, as mentioned, a very effective method is to the gather the people most knowledgeable of the event (accident or production problem) and simply ask, "Why?" five times. It is amazing what will be discovered.

Both of the specific Expectational Shop Floor and Management Myths,

> Management cares about quality only when it does not conflict with production efficiencies.
> The manufacturing facility is capable of meeting whatever specification the customer requires.

as well as the shop floor expectational myth,

> Management cares about quality only when it does not conflict with production efficiencies.

are all largely a result of critical product characteristics that were being made outside the customer's specifications.

There are a number of ways to maintain a high probability against the customer receiving product that is out of specification; however,

- Maintaining a dual specification is not one of the recommended methods.
- Internal deviations are a sure way to ensure the customer will receive out-of-specification product, and in some cases the customer is guilty of allowing the practice to perpetuate.
- The quarantine override almost always appears to the shop floor personnel as an act of desperation.

The root cause of these three myths is the lack of

- simple process capability studies that factually determine the amount of variation that is normal for a specific process so that it may be compared to the customer requirement.
- this knowledge will allow for providing the shop floor with the actual customer specification so everyone is singing from the same hymnal.

PAPER TRANSFER BELT CASE STUDY

A manufacturer of copiers designed an isoprene rubber paper feed belt critical to the smooth operation of a specific copier model. The contract to supply this belt was awarded to a New England-based corporation specializing in the manufacture of polymeric office equipment components. For approximately three years, the product was provided to the copier manufacturer free of quality problems. The copier manufacturer retired the model and instructed the supplier to place the mold used to manufacture the isoprene belt in storage.

Several years later, the copier manufacturer was in the process of designing a new copier and decided tooling costs could be avoided if the old belt configuration was designed into the new copier. The one difference would be in the belt material; the new belt would have to be manufactured using silicone rubber instead of the original isoprene rubber.

The supplier removed the mold and associated tooling from storage and, as requested, executed a sample production run of 300 molded sleeves, which were cut and trimmed to produce 1,200 finished belts. Fifty finished belts were selected at random, in sequence of manufacture, from the beginning to the end of the molding process. Measurements of three critical characteristics were recorded for the fifty samples: belt width, belt thickness, and height of a center bead on the inner diameter of the belt.

A simple arithmetic exercise indicated that a small portion of normal production would be slightly over the customer's upper specification as well as slightly under the customer's lower specification (see the Chapter 8 section on process capability studies).

The customer specification for belt width was 0.750 plus or minus 0.015 inch.

Lower specification = 0.735 inch
Upper specification = 0.765 inch

Unfortunately, the process operating with new rubber material yielded a normal variation of belt width of 0.730 to 0.770 inch. *A certain amount of product shipped to the copier company will exceed both the upper and lower customer specification.*

When the results of the study were presented to a group of managers, several representatives from the marketing department strongly suggested the belt should go into full production as the customer was behind schedule in its prototype build effort, and the few out-of-specification belts the customer might receive in every shipment would not affect the operation of the copier.

Cooler heads prevailed, and the decision was made to contact the customer and request a blueprint change for the belt width.

A conference call was initiated with the copier company design engineering group. The immediate reaction of the design engineers was to refuse the requested increase in specification in favor or reworking the tooling. It was pointed out the hard tooling could be reworked at some considerable expense, but the tooling was on consignment to the supplier as it belonged to the copier company. The cost of any rework would be the responsibility of the copier company. The teleconference ended with the customer representatives explaining they needed upper management input. Within the hour, the copier company requested a dozen belts, half of which were to be at the high of 0.770 inch and half at the low of 0.730 inch.

These belts were shipped to the copier company design engineering group; the belts were installed on test platforms and performed without difficulty. New blueprints were issued with the belt width specification (in observance of the multiple-of-five specification rule) identified at 0.750 plus or minus 0.030 inch. Several years of subsequent production ensued without customer complaint or return for dimensional problems.

If the process study had not been performed to ensure the new raw material did not introduce any unforeseen problems, it is reasonable to assume that at some point in time the copier company's inspection procedures would have discovered incoming inspection samples to have oversize or undersize widths. This would have resulted in the all-too-familiar progression of customer complaints, sales returns, increased inspection, internal rejections, rework, scrap, customer quality visits, and so on.

Truly, an ounce of prevention is worth a pound of cure.

3

Data Myths

If you cannot measure it you cannot improve it.

Lord Kelvin

Manufacturing is all about the numbers. And yet, a most insidious data myth is often shared by the shop floor and management. This particular myth is insidious for the reason that it is never verbalized; people never mention their belief that the following holds:

SHOP FLOOR AND MANAGEMENT MYTH

We don't need data to solve manufacturing process problems.

I have never once heard anyone on any shop floor or in any management group come right out and state they do not need to collect and analyze data to solve manufacturing process problems. However, this must be a widely held belief because over the years I have observed a great many people attempting to solve complex manufacturing process problems or otherwise make improvements to processes without any data collection and analysis. Therefore, it is logical that this unspoken myth exists jointly with the shop floor as well as with management.

I find this very odd because, with respect to the management component of this myth, management groups, in general, are extremely data oriented when it comes to the discipline of accounting for time, money, and resources.

Any successful manufacturing company today is managed by the numbers, such as machine efficiencies, overhead absorption, labor variances, quantities shipped, billing goals, and the like. Successful managers consistently make basic and complex business decisions based on numbers every day.

Shop floor associates, in a less-structured manner, are numbers oriented as well. Associates are in the habit of expressing their process knowledge and experiences in numbers that primarily relate to process metrics. Line speeds, tensions, pressures, temperatures, and so on are the numbers you hear going back and forth between operators on the shop floor. Unfortunately, however, when it comes to understanding more about the process of manufacturing product, neither shop floor associates nor members of management seem inclined to collect data and communicate by the numbers when dealing with process problems.

POLYMER-TO-STAINLESS STEEL SHAFT ADHESIVE CASE STUDY

The business desktop computer boom of the 1980s was accompanied by a surge in demand for computer peripheral hardware such as printers. A New England-based manufacturer had for years been enjoying a lucrative business in the manufacture of paper drive feed rollers for office copiers and faxes and realized an opportunity to provide paper drive feed rollers for printers.

Then came the advent of the personal computer for home use and the need for paper drive feed rollers surged.

Moving paper in a straight line through a copier or printer requires the paper drive rollers found in all printers, faxes, and copiers to be manufactured with a high degree of precision. These rollers typically consist of specially formulated rubber or polyurethane material bonded to a precision-machined steel shaft. The polymeric material must be capable of withstanding aggressive temperatures while maintaining a strong bond to the steel shaft.

The increased demand for rollers placed on the manufacturer resulted in the need to scale up the manufacturing process, and as so often happens in manufacturing, the increased production was accompanied by new production problems. The biggest problem came in the form of delamination of the specially formulated polyurethane and rubber rollers from the steel shafts to which they were mounted by means of specially formulated adhesives. Numerous efforts were put forth by the engineer responsible for the bonding process, and weekly meetings were conducted for the purpose of updating management regarding progress being made on this critical process problem.

The following statements are typical of what the responsible engineer offered management at the weekly update meetings:

- "The new adhesive suggested by the supplier seemed to work better for a while but, based on random sampling, the problem recently reappeared."

- "A new primer is on order, and everyone agrees this should solve the bond problem."
- "We are going to try increasing the temperature of the curing oven next. This should improve bond across the board."
- "The recent customer returns indicated poor bond was only about a quarter inch in from each end. We think this should be acceptable, and we are asking sales to request this minimum condition be accepted by the customer."
- "We think the bond is initially acceptable but weakens during our internal grinding operation due to thermal degradation. We are going to try cooling the rollers with a liquid coolant during the grinding process."

To some readers, these talking points might seem ludicrous due to the absolute lack of data; other readers may find a meeting such as I have described to be an accepted format in facilities with which they are familiar.

Eventually, the frustration level due to the litany of anecdotes totally devoid of data caused one regular member of the weekly updates to ask, as politely as possible, "What is the metric being used to determine the strength of the bond between the polymer and the steel shaft? Also, what is considered to be an adequate bond in terms of force required to separate the polymer from the steel shaft?"

An awkward silence filled the room. Bond strength data had never been quantified. Until that point, operators and inspectors "picking" at the interface of the polymer and the shaft provided the only "measurement" of bond strength. And, as may be expected, each operator, supervisor, inspector, technician, and engineer had a subjective opinion regarding what was a good bond.

A perfectly good Instron Tensile Tester was available in the R&D laboratory, and in short order samples of polymeric material were adhered to 1-inch wide templates of stainless steel for testing bond strength in terms of grams/square inch.

An adequate number of samples was produced utilizing the current manufacturing instructions and tested for bond strength on the Instron. The average bond strength of polymer to the templates was recorded to be approximately 67 grams/square inch with a normal variation equal to approximately plus and minus 23 grams/square inch. The wide distribution of data equal to plus and minus 23 grams/square inch explained the customer returns as well as why, based on random sampling procedures, the poor bond problem seemed to come and go.

Armed with the bond strength measurement method, disciplined changes could now be made to the process, such as testing new adhesive material, and informed conclusions could be derived. Within several weeks, quantifiable improvements were attained in the area of average bond strength of the polymeric material to the stainless steel shaft. Eventually, the bond strength was increased to the point that it exceeded the tensile strength of the polymer.

As mentioned, shop floor associates also fall short in the data collection arena, which often gives rise to a common shop floor myth.

Shop Floor Myth

Management doesn't listen to the operators.

To get a feel for how many conscientious shop floor associates regard data, listen to their comments at shift change or in the break room. Many of their conversations are centered on data, such as line speeds, feed rates, temperatures, and so on, but these exchanges are seldom, if ever, translated into associates acknowledging the need to collect data to communicate their process knowledge to management.

Consider an observation made by an experienced equipment operator to a supervisor as the supervisor walks through her department: "The cooling water on number seven is running as high as 75 to 80 degrees. This causes the parts to have low elongation. We need to flush out the lines!" The response can vary from, "I'll have maintenance check on it" to "We flush the lines every year at shutdown."

The associate may be very accurate in her observation, but there is a high probability that no action will result from her comments because they are anecdotal. With the exception of the water temperature readings, her concerns have not been adequately described in numerical terms. As in the case of the polymer-to-steel shaft bond study, the "low elongation" observed by the associate would need to be quantified to convert the anecdotal comment to a statement of fact, which would increase the probability of grabbing the supervisor's attention.

Statements of fact supported by data have the unique ability to bring attention to bear on a situation, whereas an anecdotal observation is an opinion, and by definition, opinions are unsubstantiated by fact and, in the real world, liable to receive little or no credibility.

As a practical matter, the manager in question may have heard a dozen anecdotes and opinions as she walked through the manufacturing area. It would be impossible to respond to all of them, and as a result, more often than not, none of them will be seriously addressed, leading to the shop floor myth.

Of course, the result of exchanges such as I have just described gives birth to the shop floor myth that *Management doesn't listen to the operators.*

I have been on hundreds of shop floors over the years, and with rare exception, the perception of the operators is that no matter how many times they point out process problems, "nothing ever gets done."

Management may very well be guilty of not providing the wherewithal for the operator to effectively communicate process knowledge by using simple data collection techniques. However, management is typically never guilty of ignoring factual ideas regarding process improvements.

The conditions that create the shop floor myth that *management doesn't listen to the operators* serves to create a second myth:

MANAGEMENT MYTH

Operators are always needlessly complaining about the process.

This is to be the expected outcome when a member of management cannot walk through the shop without multiple operators taking the opportunity to point out what they perceive to be serious process problems. Day after day, week after week, the same people are pointing out the same concerns to the same managers. Eventually, the shop floor myth that *management doesn't care about maintaining the process* and management's opinion that the *operators are always needlessly complaining about the process* both become etched in stone and coexist to everyone's detriment.

DISPELLING THE MYTHS

The root cause of both myths is quite simple. The typical shop floor associate does not express his or her process knowledge in a manner the typical manager can act on. Simply put, the operator, with the support of management, must be able to express concerns in the language of management—by the numbers.

I would like to emphasize that it is common to find manufacturing organizations that are totally numbers oriented within the realm of those data sets that are directly related to efficiencies, return on investments, overhead absorption, and so on. However, the discipline of managing the business by the numbers often does not extend to solving shop floor problems by the numbers.

As in the polymer-to-stainless steel shaft adhesive case study, members of management participate in meetings to discuss shop floor process problems and authorize suggested—and sometimes very expensive—remedies devoid of supporting data, a practice the same managers would never dream of if they were negotiating for a loan from the local commercial bank.

What chief executive officer (CEO) would consider approving a loan from a bank without any data specific to the terms of the loan? The only information made available to the CEO is the opinion of the vice president of finance that, "This is a really good bank." This is a silly premise, but it begs the question: If it is necessary for the CEO to utilize data to make critical business decisions, would it not be prudent for the CEO to set an example in process problem-solving meetings to require statements and recommendations be supported by data as well?

Similarly, production managers and shop floor supervisors use data to monitor machine efficiencies, absenteeism, tardiness, inventory levels, and so on. Yet, these same individuals often do not ask for or collect data when attempting to remedy shop floor problems related to scrap, waste, downtime, quality, and more.

Generally, in the world of manufacturing, shop floor problem solving is not data oriented. Shop floor problem solving in manufacturing is more on the order of "try this and try that." Oh, the immediate problem will likely go away—eventually. Perhaps a process change such as a new batch of raw material with a slightly different composition, due to normal variation, is introduced that offsets some other process parameter, such as feed rate, and the problem evaporates. The local problem solvers then declare victory and place blame on the raw material, which was not out of specification, just a little different due to normal variation.

The try this and try that problem-solving method will usually result in the process problem going away—eventually. Even the blind squirrel finds the occasional acorn. In this case, the culprit has been identified as the raw material based on anecdotal evidence, and scarce resources will be dispatched to find a "better raw material."

Process problems are not solved unless the root cause of the problem can be quantified, and this requires following a problem-solving discipline that includes the collection and the simple analysis of data. Consider how many times a day throughout American manufacturing facilities a supervisor will drop tagged samples of product on the desk of an engineer and announce, "We have a problem on number fifteen injection molding line."

To the engineer's question, "What kind of problem?" posed to the back of the receding supervisor comes the answer, "A big one!" Or, sometimes the answer will be "voids" or "excessive flash," each of which of course is a symptom of the problem, not *the* problem. Problems should never be presented without some supporting data, and a random sample tagged with a description "excessive flash" does not qualify as data.

Consider the previous example in which the operator made the observation that, "The cooling water on number seven is running as high as 75 to 80 degrees. This causes the parts to have low elongation." The term *low elongation* needs to be defined numerically by the operator or at least with the operator's involvement. It would be a simple and inexpensive exercise to direct the operator to select, at random, twenty-five samples during the time she observes the water temperature indicator at 80 degrees or lower. Those twenty-five samples can then be measured on an elongation tester and recorded on a histogram.

A histogram of percentage elongation similar to the histogram previously described in Chapter 2 will serve several purposes:

- The operator will clearly see that the product characteristic elongation varies.
- The center, low, and high points of the histogram can be compared to the nominal, low, and high engineering specification, and it can be determined if the elongation is within the desired specification.
- If the histogram upper and lower measurements fall outside the customer specifications, management has acquired valuable process information. If, on the other hand, the histogram falls well within the specification the operator, by default, the entire shop floor now knows the "low" chill water temperature does not cause a low elongation problem.
- The operator now recognizes the histogram as a simple shop floor problem-solving tool that can be used to effectively communicate her observations to management. And, more important, management does listen to the operators when their information is quantified.
- The next time she has a concern about a particular product characteristic, the operator can collect some data, put it into histogram form, and present it along with her comments.
- As a result of the usual shop floor communication network, operators who bring a concern to management will begin to accompany that concern with data.

- Regardless of the outcome of the elongation study, the first step has been taken in dispelling the myths that *management doesn't care about the process* and *the operators are always needlessly complaining about the process.*

THE REALITY OF COLLECTING SHOP FLOOR DATA

The three manufacturing myths discussed thus far in this chapter all concern the collection of process or product data. All three myths can be dispelled by analyzing data. In manufacturing industries, data is the great slayer of myths. However, data needs to be collected, and the best resource for collecting data is the shop floor associates. The difficulty, as most people will attest, is the fact that the typical operator despises the idea of collecting data. This is a reality I have experienced on every shop floor.

There are a number of reasons why manufacturing shop floor associates are averse to collecting data:

- Mandates to collect data normally come from management as a result of a significant customer complaint, a customer return, a costly shop floor error, and so on. The sole purpose of the mandated data collection is most often directed at having a record that some action was taken to prevent a recurrence of the complaint, return, or error.
- For example, an entire shift's output of one line was determined to be scrap because the cure temperature was set significantly lower than the work instruction minimum setting. Therefore, going forward each operator was required to record, on the appropriate form, the cure temperature once an hour.
  - For the first week, the forms were gathered at the end of each shift, carefully read by the shift supervisor, who signed his name in full to indicate he had verified the data. The production clerk then picked up the forms and brought them to the production manager on a daily basis; the production manager ensured the data had been recorded and properly signed off by the supervisor.
  - The second week, the forms were gathered at the end of each shift, and the supervisor then *initialed* the forms, without reading them. The production clerk picked up the forms and delivered

them to the production manager, who set them aside on his desk without verifying the data or the supervisor's signature.

- After several weeks, the forms were filled out by the operators, who began to notice the supervisors no longer reviewed them, and the production clerk ceased to gather them on a daily basis. The forms began to pile up on the operators' workbenches and gather dust and eventually were discarded. No one noticed.
- At some point, the operators stopped filling out the forms, and no one noticed.

This scenario is played out repeatedly in manufacturing. The mandated data collection could be related to

- Quality: Select one random sample every 30 minutes; measure and record the cross-hatched diameter.
- Inventory: At the beginning and end of each shift, measure the amount of polymer in the silo.
- Process Parameters: Record the pH of the chemical bath every hour.
- Productivity: Record the amount of time it takes to change the die on the 20-ton press.

Regardless of the mandate, it most often plays out as receiving a great deal of attention for a brief period of time. The attention wanes to the point that the data sheets are no longer collected. The data sheets build up and are finally discarded; the operators eventually cease collecting the data. Then, a new data collection mandate is issued, and the cycle begins again.

The rules for collecting shop floor data should be as follows:

- With rare exception, shop floor data should be collected for the sole purpose of identifying the root cause of a shop floor problem.
- The operators should be totally familiarized with the reason they are being involved in the data collection effort.
- A finite amount of data needs to be identified.
- The results of the data should always be shared with the individuals who participated in collecting the data.

For example, there is a recognized difficulty in maintaining a consistent thickness on the GM dash panel connectors due to excessive flash. The first-, second-, and third-shift operators on this line are asked to select one random sample every hour. We would like each operator involved to tag each part and record on the tag the thickness of the part and the time the measurement was taken. We only need twenty-four parts for this initial phase of the study.

Engineering will analyze the data, and a brief meeting will be held with each operator to review the results and discuss the next step in the investigation.

In summary, process problems cannot be efficiently addressed without data, and the best resource for collecting data is the shop floor associates. However, the shop floor associates must understand the reason for the data collection exercise, the exercise must have a definite end, and most important, the results must be shared with all of the participants.

MISUSE OF DATA

As with any tool, data can be misused. One of the most damaging misuses of data is its application to the cost-accounting component commonly referred to as the "allowable scrap factor." For those readers who are familiar with manufacturing organizations that have evolved beyond the use of the allowable scrap concept, I would offer a definition of the term.

When the professionals in the cost-accounting departments of many manufacturing facilities determine the sales price of a manufactured product, they take into account the cost of raw materials, the cost of direct and indirect labor, the cost of overhead, which would include such items as the expense of heating and lighting the facility and the like. And, of course, the required profit margin is included because everyone is interested in making money. Finally, an allowable scrap factor is included in order to pass on to the customer the cost of anticipated scrap that will be made during the manufacturing process.

The anticipated scrap has become widely known as the allowable scrap factor. A 5 percent allowable scrap factor is rather common, although I have worked in several processes that have been assigned allowable scrap factors as high as 10 percent. The multiple-of-five specification rule seems to have spilled over into the accounting departments of the world with regard to allowable scrap factors.

The very term *allowable scrap factor* carries an offensive connotation and is a result of a warped perception of the original intent of the concept.

The warped perception for an allowable scrap factor of 5 percent can be defined as follows:

- As an operator, I understand I am "allowed" to make a certain level of scrap.
- As a production manager, I should be pleased if a job does not exceed 5 percent scrap; therefore, I see no need in trying to improve the scrap experience for this product.
- As a CEO, I should distribute bonuses at the end of the year if our overall scrap experience was no greater than 5 percent.

The existence of an allowable scrap factor gives rise to the following myth/shibboleth:

Management is happy if scrap does not exceed the allowable level.

All the managers I know would be happy if there were *no* additional costs due to scrap of any kind—allowable or otherwise. However, most people rise to a certain level of minimum expectation, and if management sends the false signal that 5 or 10 percent scrap is acceptable, that is exactly what they will get in the long term. Of course, most senior members of management reinforce this false expectation by calling meetings and asking direct questions only when the scrap level exceeds the allowable limit.

The mindset seems to be if we are exceeding our allowable scrap, we are losing money. Read that as we, not the customer, are now absorbing the cost of some of the scrap. We are losing money, and that is unacceptable.

At this point, I state the obvious: Any time a company is producing scrap, the company is losing money.

ALLOWABLE SCRAP CASE STUDY

Due to competitive pressures, a Midwestern furniture manufacturer with a number of facilities located around the country launched a companywide effort in the mid-1990s aimed at lowering the cost of all aspects of manufacturing.

One of the company's larger spring-manufacturing facilities located in the Southeast that had a history of generating excessive scrap was directed by corporate to submit a written plan that would result in lowering its scrap rate to the allowable 10 percent. The manager of the facility under discussion mandated that each morning the general supervisor was to calculate the combined scrap rate for the previous three shifts. If the combined scrap rate for all three shifts exceeded the allowable 10 percent, the cause of the excessive scrap was to be identified and presented to the plant manager at the 10:00 a.m. production meeting.

The first morning after the mandate was issued to identify the cause of any 24-hour cumulative scrap rate in excess of 10 percent, the general supervisor was able to report a scrap level of 4.8 percent. Everyone was quite pleased with the report, which resulted in a very short production meeting.

The second morning, however, the reported scrap rate was 12.2%, but no single cause for the excessive scrap could be identified by the general supervisor. The plant manager would not accept the absence of a cause and insisted that the next time the scrap level exceeded the minimum a root cause *must* accompany the report. The general supervisor was informed clearly that it was his responsibility to work with the three shift supervisors to assign a cause to any cumulative scrap rate in excess of 10 percent.

The general supervisor, in turn, berated the three shift supervisors and informed them he was not going to another morning production meeting without a reason for scrap in excess of 10%. The supervisors attempted in vain to explain that, try as they might, they were not always able to clearly identify a single major cause of any high-scrap 24-hour period. As a matter of fact, it was rather seldom they could, with certainty, point to excessive scrap resulting from the output of an inexperienced operator or a component malfunction on one of the many spring-forming machines.

The supervisor's frustrations rose on a par with the tensions at the 10:00 a.m. production meetings when, on most occasions, root causes for excessive scrap were not available for presentation to the plant manager.

Finally, with a little coaching, the second-shift supervisor looked at data representing scrap levels for the previous 30 days and discovered the average scrap level for that period was just under 8.5%. Of course, an average of 8.5% would imply that some days would be higher than 8.5%, and other days would be lower than 8.5%.

The same data was then laid out in histogram form (see Figure 3.1). The histogram clearly demonstrated a bell-shaped pattern. At risk of repetition, the bell-shaped pattern indicates normal variation.

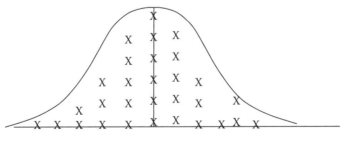

3.5　4.5　5.5　6.5　7.5　8.5%　9.5　10.5　11.5　12.5 13.5%

FIGURE 3.1
Histogram 30 days' percentage of scrap springs.

Allow me to put this statement into context with regard to the scrap experience at this particular spring-manufacturing plant. This histogram indicates that, under normal conditions, this process, which, as explained in Chapter 1, would consist of the equipment, raw material, people, and methods, will generate on the average 8.5% scrap. Also, on any given day it would be perfectly normal for this facility to experience scrap as low as 3.5% or as high as 13.5%.

Considering neither the general supervisor nor the three shift supervisors could purchase raw material with less variation or spend capital money that might result in less equipment variation or reduce the variation of methods by rewriting the work instructions created by industrial engineering and so on, they could not have a positive impact on the variation that was normal to the process. And, without reducing the normal variation, the facility could expect to continue experiencing random days with scrap as high as 13.5%.

It is axiomatic in industry that only management can provide or improve the four elements of the process, which is the only method of affecting variation that is normal to a process.

The second-shift supervisor, without using anything more complicated than a pencil and a piece of graph paper, had demonstrated the scrap data was "normal." The supervisors could not identify causes for high scrap for any single 24-hour period because no identifiable causes existed; scrap as high as 13.5 percent was perfectly normal for this process as it was presently configured.

When this information was presented to management, it was met with a degree of disbelief. It required an analogy be drawn between the facility's scrap and a dice or "craps" table at a casino. Players rolling dice at a craps table win or lose as a function of naturally random variation. Specifically, if one hundred rolls of the dice were recorded and plotted in a histogram, the shape, assuming the dice had not been tampered with, would be in the form of the bell curve. This natural curve of one hundred rolls of the dice is the result of very simple rules of probability. There are two dice involved in one single roll. Combinations of the two dice determine if the person rolling the dice wins or loses.

Table 3.1 represents the probability of the combinations resulting when two honest dice are cast. The only combination that will result in a *two* is when the dice come up *one* and one. There is a very low probability of getting a *two*. On the other hand, the number *seven* can be attained with six combinations. There is a much higher probability of rolling a *seven*.

At the casino dice tables, if a person rolls a *two* on his or her first cast, that person must roll a *two*, which is his or her point, again before the person rolls a *seven*. If the person rolls a *seven* before rolling his or her point—in this case a *two*—the person loses or "craps out."

Referencing Table 3.1, it is easy to see the odds are against that person rolling a *three* one more time before crapping out by rolling a *seven* and losing money.

TABLE 3.1

Histogram of Honest Dice

Number Rolled	Combination				
2	1&1				
3	1&2	2&1			
4	1&3	3&1	2&2		
5	1&4	4&1	2&3	3&2	
6	1&5	5&1	2&4	4&2	3&3
7	1&6	6&1	2&4	4&2	3&4	4&3
8	2&6	6&2	3&5	5&3	4&4
9	3&6	6&3	4&5	5&4	
10	4&6	6&4	5&5		
11	5&6	6&5			
12	6&6				

If Table 3.1, is turned on its side, the similarity between the bell curve formed by the probability of winning (or losing) at the dice tables and the second-shift supervisor's histogram is obvious. The variation formed by the historical scrap data indicates the scrap data is a function of normal, random variation in the same way normal, random variation controls the dice.

It took a little time for management to accept the basic fact that the occasional scrap experience greater than 10%, and as high as 13.5%, was a result of the normal, random variation of the spring-manufacturing process. The variation of the raw material combined with the variation of the equipment line speed, tensions, tooling, and so on were, more than likely, major contributors to the scrap experience, and the operators and supervisors were powerless to reduce the variation of the process.

Only management could improve the scrap performance because only management can make the kinds of process changes that would be necessary to do so.

The good news is that using the histogram in Figure 3.1, the management team, going forward, could track the success or lack of success of process improvements the team chose to make.

IN CONCLUSION

I cannot overemphasize the importance of data with respect to breaking down barriers within management groups as well as the barriers that typically exist between management and the shop floor. The average manufacturing facility does not need an in-house statistician or a hierarchy of

Six Sigma belts to collect data and use simple, time-proven techniques to solve shop floor problems, reduce scrap, improve quality, and become generally more competitive. The father of statistical process control, Dr. W. A. Shewhart, said it best: "The fact that the criterion which we happen to use has a fine ancestry of highbrow statistical theorems does not justify its use. Such justification must come from empirical evidence that it works."

4

Our Process Is Different

Differences challenge assumptions.

Anne Wilson Schaef

Solving problems in manufacturing requires a lot of discipline and a little bit of science. I use the term *science* in context of the definition that science is "knowledge, as of facts or principles; knowledge gained by systematic study."[*]

Unfortunately, neither discipline nor science is used in many companies on a regular basis to address manufacturing problems. All too often, when faced with a process problem during a shift, the operators, due to real or imagined production pressures, try to solve the product problem by means of manipulating process parameters.

Often, when an operator observes an unacceptable product characteristic, the operator will attempt to correct the problem by adjusting a process parameter. If, after a brief period of time, the product problem does not improve, the operator will very likely return the adjusted process parameter to its original position and adjust a different process parameter. This method of trying to solve a process problem could go on for hours until by the end of the shift the problem solver might not be able to remember what had or had not been tried. And, the oncoming shift very likely will begin their own similar "poke-and-hope" efforts. I do not mean to criticize the valiant efforts of shop floor associates, but the problem-solving methods they employ are, in general, the result of a lack of management-provided training in more effective problem-solving methods.

With respect to problem-solving techniques used by supervisors and other members of management groups, one of two situations prevails in many manufacturing facilities:

---

[*] http://dictionary.reference.com/browse/science?s=t

a. The management group has not received training in proven problem-solving methods.
b. The management group has had the training, but they consciously choose not to apply the methods they have learned.

At this late date in our manufacturing evolution, I find that most management groups have been exposed to appropriate problem-solving training, but they often just choose not to engage the tools they have learned as a result of two management myths.

Management Myth

We don't have the time or the available people to follow a rigid discipline—we have to solve the problem ... now!

Management Myth

Our process is different; many of the problem-solving techniques we learned do not apply here.

With respect to the first of these two management myths—*We don't have the time or the available people to follow a rigid discipline—we have to solve the problem ... now!*—identifying the root cause of a process problem should not be a solitary endeavor; usually, the investment of having several people work on a serious production problem is a wise investment. The root cause of a problem could be the result of raw material, equipment, operator technique, prescribed methods, or a combination of two or more of these process elements. It would be a rare individual who would have the expertise in all four of the process components plus extensive hands-on process experience, all of which would be necessary to efficiently solve a serious and costly process problem. In the absence of such a person, the only alternative is to bring together a cross section of several individuals for a specific period of time in order to engage in a synergistic problem-solving session. This group should *always* include at least one process-knowledgeable shop floor associate.

Equipment operators and assistants may not understand as much about the process technology as members of the engineering group, but they can often make up for a lack of in-depth technological expertise with their nuanced understanding of the process in which they spend as much as 30% of their waking hours.

Volumes have been written offering detailed instructions on how to use the basic group problem-solving tools, such as brainstorming, Pareto charting, failure mode effect analysis, and others, and going into detailed application of these techniques is beyond the scope of this book. More information on these topics is offered as suggested reading material in the Bibliography.

INSULATION VOIDS CASE STUDY

A major Midwestern wire and cable manufacturer was experiencing costly scrap and customer returns due to voids in the insulation of wire that was engineered for application in the high-speed telecommunication industry. This was, by definition, a sporadic problem.

The presence of voids would be identified by an operator; engineers or supervisors and the observer would recommend changes to heat profiles, line speed or tensions, and so on, and the problem would go away. Victory would be declared, and the process parameter change that resulted in success was recorded and incorporated in the standard procedure documentation. After some time, the voids would reappear; engineers or supervisors would initiate new settings (make adjustments) until the voids were eliminated, and documentation would be updated until the voids reappeared and on and on. I am confident this scenario is familiar to many readers.

As happens with many sporadic manufacturing problems, this one reached critical mass as a result of a customer mandate to correct the void problem or risk losing the account. The customer demand, of course, resulted in a strong upper management emphasis being placed on solving the problem for the last time.

Ironically, one engineer expressed his newfound sense of urgency with the following statement: "Over the months we have tried everything to no avail, so as a last resort, we have decided to use the more disciplined approach."

A group of five individuals was scheduled for a 1-hour meeting in the conference room. The group consisted of an engineer, a supervisor, an inspector, and two extruder operators.

A brainstorming session was conducted by a coordinator, and raw material was scored as a principal contributor to the problem of voids.

The coordinator asked, "Why is the raw material a problem?"

An extruder operator responded, "It changed about 6 months ago."

"Why did it change?"

"It's a two-part polymer, and we have to blend it on the floor now."

"Why is that a change?"

"It used to come in blended but now it comes in unblended."

"Why does it now come to you unblended?"

"Purchasing changed suppliers."

"Why did purchasing change the suppliers?"

"I was told they got a better price."

Everyone was thanked for their participation, and the meeting was concluded in a little more than 30 minutes.

It was, in fact, true that purchasing had changed suppliers to attain a more favorable price, but the trade-off was the need to blend two polymers in a predetermined proportion by weight. A small Sears cement mixer had been purchased and set up close to the extruder line that produced the subject wire. A scale had been purchased so the operators could weigh the two polymers according to the required proportions that had been posted on a corkboard above the workstation bench. No specific instructions were provided for how long the polymers were to be blended, and rotational speed of the cement mixer was not identified. The scale was not calibrated, and although the proportions of the two polymers were clearly defined, the size of a batch was left to the judgment of the operators. Reason would dictate significant variation was being introduced to the raw material due to variation of the blending process, possibly resulting in insulation voids.

A quantity of blended raw material was ordered from the original supplier, introduced to the process, and carefully monitored for several shifts to ensure the absence of voids. The next day, instructions were issued to the purchasing department to return to the former supplier that provided the blended product.

This case study is not an unusual example of the positive results that can often be attained by bringing a group of process-knowledgeable individuals together. The brainstorm technique is very effective in creating consensus regarding what the group believes to be a direction to take. In this case, the direction was clearly to take a hard look at the raw material.

Once the raw material direction was determined, the coordinator merely asked "Why?" a number of times. The rule of thumb is to ask "Why?" five times, and the direction to take will be further refined, which is exactly what this group experienced.

Asking five people to convene in the conference room achieved in a little more than 30 minutes what had not been achieved in months of trial-and-error troubleshooting.

Of course, the two operators were not producing product during the time they were in the conference room adding their knowledge of the extrusion process to the problem-solving process, but neither were they on their respective extrusion lines making product with voids in the insulation.

MANAGEMENT MYTH: OUR PROCESS IS DIFFERENT

I have experienced the success of these very basic problem-solving tools in industries ranging from a mushroom farm to one of the world's largest fiber-optic cable manufacturers. Yet, often, when I mention how useful these tools can be, I get a response such as the following:

We've tried those techniques, and we have found some of them work very well. However, we have never had success with these customer Six Sigma requirements. We have tried, but we find the Six Sigma requirements time consuming, expensive, and inconclusive. The results we get never reflect our product. We've seen examples of success with Six Sigma techniques in other industries, but they do not work here because our process is different.

This is a difficult position for a supplier company to find itself in view of the fact that the manufacturing environment today is becoming increasingly demanding as customers adopt the philosophies of Six Sigma.

One of the more demanding requirements, and the requirement with which many manufacturers struggle, calls for suppliers to demonstrate that critical characteristics be manufactured not only within specification but also *well within specification*. Without going into what many people would term the statistical voodoo of Six Sigma, I would like to offer a simple clarification of this requirement.

Six Sigma requirements, simply stated, mean that

- When the normal variation of a product characteristic is centered at the customer's nominal, the total width of the normal variation (bell-shaped curve) may not exceed more than 75 percent of the customer's total specification.
- If these criteria are met, the product characteristic is said to be capable with a capability index of 1.33.
- The 1.33 index number is the ratio of 100 percent of the specification divided by the allowable; 100%/75% = 1.33 (see Figure 4.1).
- This ratio of normal variation to specification is determined by a capability study.

The basic concept is simple; however, there are many nuances involved in the execution.

One of the nuances that cause such consternation to suppliers of Six Sigma-oriented customers is the requirement to demonstrate that the center of the bell-shaped curve was not changing or shifting due to unknown causes during the capability study. If the center of the bell-shaped curve was shifting due to unknown reasons during the study, the process is said to be "not stable." And, in order for a product characteristic to be capable, it must first be stable (see Figure 4.2).

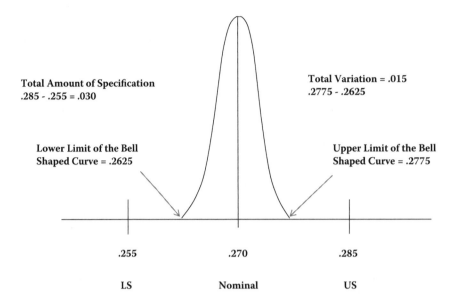

FIGURE 4.1
Six Sigma concept of capability.

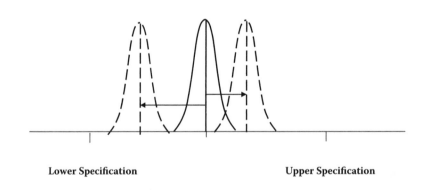

FIGURE 4.2
Process average shifts or instability.

The following is a quick review: Any customer who requires adherence to Six Sigma concepts wants to see an analysis of product data that indicates

- The product characteristic is stable; the center of the bell-shaped curve is not changing or shifting due to unknown causes.
- The product characteristic is capable, the bell-shaped curve, when stable takes up no more than 75 percent of the specification.
- And, again, this is all factually demonstrated by means of a process capability study.

For further information, see the section in Chapter 8 on process capability studies.

In return for my not going into all the details and statistical formulas and justifications for the simplistic explanations already provided, take a leap of faith now and accept the following statement: The success of any capability study depends on the *range*, or the *numerical difference*, between subsequent samples selected during the study. Stated differently, the time that lapses between the selection of consecutive samples is critical. Many companies over the years have "failed" customer-required capability studies, and lost business, because the criticality of the time between the selection of subsequent samples was not fully understood.

I cannot overemphasize the importance of the range between consecutive data points, and without getting too "statistical." In the next section, I will attempt to explain why this range is so important.

THE CONTROL CHART

One important requirement of a Six Sigma capability study is to demonstrate the product characteristic under study is stable. The only effective method of accomplishing this is to provide a control chart (see the section on control charts in Chapter 8). Think of the control chart as the bell-shaped curve turned on its side with calculated control chart limits extending across the page. These calculated control chart limits represent the estimate of long-term normal variation of the product characteristic being evaluated (see Figure 4.3). The calculated control chart limits, representing an estimate of long-term product variation, are based on the range

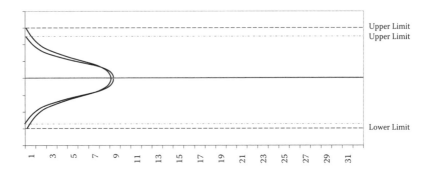

FIGURE 4.3
Control chart. The bell-shaped curve turned on its side.

of consecutive samples selected over a relatively short period of time such as one shift.

Think of a control chart like this:

- The customer wants a level of confidence the product characteristic is stable and, over the long run, capable of remaining well within the customer's upper and lower specifications.
- No one knows the future, but we have learned that we can take a minimum number of samples over a relatively *short* period of time, such as an entire shift or perhaps two or three shifts, in an effort to estimate the normal variation we can expect over a much *longer* period of time—weeks, months, or until the process undergoes a change such as a different raw material supplier is activated.
- To derive this *long*-term estimate of normal variation for a product characteristic, we use the *short*-term range between consecutive samples and apply some simple arithmetic developed in the 1930s.
- The simple arithmetic provides us valid limits of the long-term bell-shaped curve, and we extend these limits, centered about the grand average of the selected samples, across the page. We then plot the raw data of the individual measured samples from beginning to end in the order they were selected (see Figure 4.4).

There are a number of control charts, and I have just described the individuals control chart, which I recommend in all but a few rare cases. Unfortunately, many manufacturing companies use various types of control charts, which, without an in-depth understanding of several

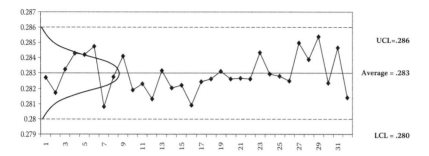

FIGURE 4.4
Control chart. The bell-shaped curve turned on its side.

statistical concepts, can cause a great deal of confusion and expensive, wrong conclusions.

The pattern made by the data points on the individuals control chart indicates the stability of the product characteristic. There are a number of rules that are applied to the patterns. For instance, a single data point outside either the upper or lower control limit is an indication of instability (Figure 4.5). Refer to Chapter 8 for a list of the four most commonly applied rules.

> Stability Rule 1: If a single data point falls outside either limit, it is an indication of product instability. It is an indication the bell-shaped curve has shifted in the direction of the errant data point (see Figure 4.5).

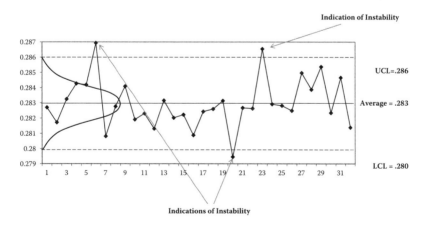

FIGURE 4.5
Control chart indicating instability.

INJECTION MOLDING CASE STUDY

A supplier to the automotive industry in the Northeast was aggressively pursuing favored supplier status with one of Detroit's Big Three automobile companies. For those younger readers, that would be GM, Ford, and Chrysler, not Toyota, Nissan, and Kia.

In order to qualify for this supplier program, the company was required to perform a process capability study. The study was required in order to quantify the degree of dimensional variation of several critical characteristics of an injection-molded part that was about the diameter and thickness of a dime. Briefly stated, the automotive company required the supplier company to demonstrate its process was stable and capable.

- **Stable:** Center of the bell-shaped curve was not unpredictably shifting.
- **Capable:** The bell-shaped curve, when centered at the customer nominal, took up no more than 75 percent of the total specification.

The injection-molding process consisted of a five-cavity mold with approximately a 12-second cycle time. Five molded pieces were ejected approximately every 12 seconds.

The Quality Department instructed the operators to select five consecutive samples ejected from cavity number one every 15 minutes until fifteen groups of five had been collected. The thickness of each of the five samples was to be measured by an inspector and recorded for the purpose of creating an average chart and a range chart.

The average chart would be used for the purpose of understanding the variation of the averages (sometimes referred to as the mean) of the groups of five samples, and the range chart would be for the purpose of understanding the variation of the ranges (the largest diameter in each group of five minus the smallest diameter in each group of five) of each group of five samples.

The data collection went smoothly, and everyone was quite happy that the thickness of all the collected samples was well within the customer's specification.

The Quality Department performed the required arithmetic, which resulted in the required average chart and a range chart (see Figure 4.6).

Important Point: The instability rule 1 previously discussed for the individuals chart also applies to the average and range charts.

It is difficult to describe the disappointment, confusion, and consternation that ran through this facility when the Quality Department informed management that the capability study clearly indicated that, although all the measurements were well within the customer's specification limits, the process was totally unstable. There were numerous violations of rule 1. Data points were outside the upper and lower control limits on the average chart.

The supplier company had been providing this part to the automotive industry for years and had never experienced a complaint or return due to

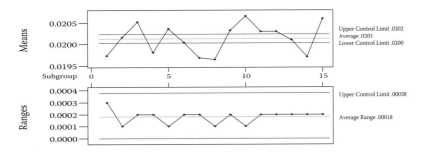

FIGURE 4.6
Molded thickness capability study.

out-of-specification thickness, yet it just now discovered the process was not stable.

Management instructed the responsible departments to perform the study again. The study was repeated, and the results of the second study were identical to the first study. The results of this capability study could not possibly be sent to the customer. The management mandate came down: "Spare no expense but find and remove the cause of the instability."

As a result of brainstorming sessions, the platens of the injection-molding machine were ground down; the study was performed again with the same results—instability.

Over several weeks, different lubricants were trialed, cooling lines were flushed, mandates to keep windows closed were issued, electrical loads were investigated, and more. Every time the process capability study was repeated, the results were the same (refer to Figure 4.6). Specifically, data points were above and below the control chart limits indicating instability in spite of the fact that all the measured thickness values were well within the customer specification.

The cry went up: This Six Sigma concept does not apply to our process because *our process is different*. Outside assistance was requested and provided.

Within minutes of reviewing the data and the charts, the suggestion was made that selecting a sample from cavity one every hour would be more appropriate. One group of five samples would then be created every 5 hours instead of the previous plan that selected one sample every 12 seconds, which created a group of five samples within a single minute.

It was suggested the problem with the previous studies was that a number of data points were falling outside the control chart limits indicating instability because the control chart limits were artificially narrow.

- The control chart limits are a result of the average range value.
- If the average range is very small, the control chart limits of both the average and the range charts will be very narrow.

In order to perform a process capability study, it is necessary to apply knowledge of the process before selecting samples from the process. For instance, anyone with knowledge of an injection-molding process with a cycle time of 12 seconds would understand that five samples selected from one cavity over a period of 1 minute would demonstrate virtually no variation. It would not be logical to believe the amount of thickness variation within five samples, each roughly the size of a thick dime, from the output of one cavity during a period of 1 minute would be useful in predicting the thickness of this part over a period of several months or a year.

- How much variation would there be in the few grams of raw material required to make five samples from the output of 1 minute of this molding process?
- How much tool wear would be experienced over a period of 1 minute?
- How much variation could be introduced by the operator over a period of 1 minute?

I submit you do not need to be an expert in injection molding to answer these three questions with the answers "none," "none," and "none."

And, if there is virtually no variation in the process elements during 1 minute, there would be virtually no thickness range within the five samples taken from that single cycle, and the control chart limits would be artificially narrow, giving false indications of instability. Perhaps the *only* range that would register would be the measurement error inherent in the micrometer method of measuring the thickness of the parts. There is no way the amount of range within five samples from 1 minute of this molding process could possibly be used to estimate the long-term thickness variation for purposes of providing a valid capability study.

It was suggested that one random sample from the output of cavity one be selected every hour until fifteen groups of five samples each over a period of three shifts had been collected for the development of a new average and range chart combination (see Figure 4.7). This control chart indicates the thickness of the injection-molded product was both stable and capable.

A PROCESS IS A PROCESS

It would be natural for a manufacturing company to take a great deal of pride in its technology and the product that results from its efforts. But, whether a company is making fiber-optic connectors or concrete telephone poles processes all share a common foundation. Each one consists of people, raw material, equipment, and methods.

The people, raw material, equipment, and methods of making fiber-optic connectors may be very different from the people, raw material, equipment, and methods of making concrete telephone poles. However, to be

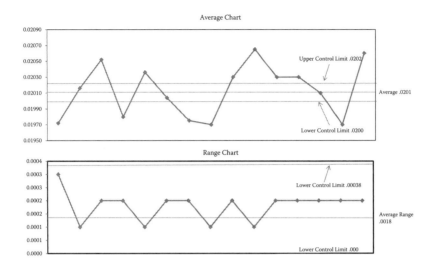

FIGURE 4.7
Molded thickness capability study I.

competitive in today's marketplace, both manufacturers must understand that the variation introduced to the product is the result of the variation in the four components of the process.

In this sense, all processes are the same, and the variation of the processes can be understood using common tools provided *specific process knowledge* is taken into consideration.

Before a capability study is performed, it is necessary to develop a consensus, based on process knowledge and experience, regarding what relatively short period of time (hours, a full shift, three shifts, 2 days) is necessary to estimate normal variation over a relatively long period of time (weeks, months, a year). For example, it might take several days before die wear in a copper wire-drawing process will affect the product. However, it may take only hours before die wear in a stainless steel wire-drawing process may affect the product.

Too often, manufacturing facilities attempt to satisfy a Six Sigma requirement without being fully conversant in the nuances of a number of the tools required. Unfortunately, with respect to Six Sigma, one tool does not apply to all processes, and this gives rise to the management myth that *our process is different.*

Experience dictates that an extremely reliable source of specific process knowledge can be acquired by involving the operators in the design of the process capability study. Once they have an understanding of the need to identify normal variation, they can be very instrumental in suggesting how to construct the sample plan.

Operators should be fully involved in the planning and execution of a capability study.

There is a shop floor myth that is a variation of the management myth that *our process is different*:

Shop Floor Myth

My process setup is the best.

OPERATORS

Operators are an important and integral part of any manufacturing process. The typical equipment operator in manufacturing considers his or her process to be very different from all other processes in the manufacturing world. The operator also tends to believe his or her particular modification to the standard procedure is very different, and much more effective, than the modifications applied to the standard procedure by colleagues.

In spite of what many management groups believe, standard procedures, work instructions, standard manufacturing practices, and so on are, in fact, seldom followed to the letter by shop floor associates. In some organizations, I find it to be more of an open secret that shop floor associates do not follow standard procedures, and this open secret prevails as long as the process keeps producing quality product at an acceptable efficiency level accompanied by scrap that does not exceed the allowable scrap level established by the cost accountants. In some organizations, I have recognized management's interest in following procedures only becomes acute just prior to an ISO (International Organization for Standardization) 9000 audit, customer visit, or some other outside stimuli.

The fact that standard procedures developed by engineering, and the research and development (R&D) professionals, are not religiously followed on the shop floor is most often the result of the process that does not perform as well in production as it performed during the R&D trials, which, of course, led to the new process being released to manufacturing. Many organizations expect the manufacturing department to produce product that will meet a customer's stability and capability requirements without first requiring engineering and R&D to demonstrate the stability and capability of the qualifying trials prior to releasing the newly developed process to the manufacturing department.

A new process is developed with a great deal of mechanical, chemical, electrical, and other specialized engineering expertise. Whether these professionals develop the new process in a pilot process located in a laboratory environment or on the shop floor using production equipment, their technological expertise is undoubtedly greater than the technological expertise of the shop floor associates. Also, an R&D trial that is determined to be successful is usually of a much shorter duration than a normal production run.

To summarize, it has been known that a group of professionals, after a number of failed trials, announce a short run to be successful and declare a new manufacturing process, complete with a standard procedure that worked well in an R&D environment, is now ready for normal production.

Unfortunately, too many times a new process transitions from R&D to *research and production,* leaving all the wrinkles to be ironed out by supervisors and associates while they try valiantly to maintain delivery schedules without exceeding the allowable scrap level. At the very least, this is when the shop floor production supervisor and the shop floor associates begin to experience process behavior not experienced in the short-term R&D development effort, and they begin to compensate by making adjustments.

There are a number of reasons the production department might not be as successful as the R&D department in producing quality product over time. Different raw material batches might demonstrate different properties of hardness, elongation, melt index, and so on, which will cause the process to change when a new batch of material is introduced to the process. R&D may have only used one batch of material in its successful trial. The same could be said with respect to various electrical loads between one shift and another, which could cause erratic behavior that was not experienced on a first shift during the R&D successful trial.

Different examples would apply to different processes, but the point is that a short-term laboratory trial is not necessarily robust enough to justify a new process be released to production.

This practice, which I am familiar with on three different continents, is common throughout manufacturing industries, and it leads to institutionalizing the need for shop floor associates and supervisors to make adjustments in order to produce quality product with reasonable efficiencies to compensate for processes that demonstrate a lack of stability over time for all the reasons stated and then some. It would be so much more effective to require the engineering and R&D departments to qualify a successful trial in terms of stability and capability in order to ensure that critical characteristics have a better chance of meeting the requirements the customers expect under normal manufacturing conditions.

It is important to understand that when a process that is inherently unstable or not capable reaches manufacturing, the supervisors and shop floor associates will eventually identify product that does not meet specification. When this occurs, it seems to be a natural phenomenon that the operators believe it is up to them to make compensatory adjustments.

Compensatory adjustments can have a short-term benefit, but in the long term, they are always detrimental to the competitiveness of the organization.

The belief that it is perfectly acceptable for equipment operators to make adjustments to their processes during their shift eventually evolves to the practice of each operator setting up the process according to the way he or she believes is most effective. This is manifested by a shop floor myth among equipment operators: *My process setup is the best.* This can cause difficulties on several levels.

MATTRESS UNIT CASE STUDY

The mattresses the average family purchases are finely upholstered by companies with recognizable household names. It is not widely known among consumers that the spring assemblies that are upholstered are highly engineered units manufactured by companies other than the upholsterers.

Several upholstering companies were having difficulty processing shipments of spring assemblies through their automatic upholstering equipment because the lengths of the spring assemblies within a shipment were very different. The received units were always within specification, but the range of the spring assembly lengths varied from minimum to maximum.

This variation in the spring assembly lengths was causing scrap at the upholsterers and the need to shut down and recalibrate the upholstering equipment to compensate for the variation in lengths. Sometime after the equipment was recalibrated and when again processing the spring units without difficulty, the length of the units would change, creating scrap and the need to shut down and recalibrate the equipment again.

Eventually, the upholsterers compensated for the inconsistent incoming length of the spring assemblies by inspecting and segregating the assemblies by length. This was an expensive operation and was being charged back to the supplier.

To make a reasonably long story short, a capability study was eventually performed at the spring assembly supplier's facility. It was quickly determined that a number of operators had developed their own setup methods that resulted in noticeable differences in the spring assembly lengths depending on which operator made the unit. Everyone was prodded back to setting up the process according to the standard operating procedure, and the problem at the upholstering customers evaporated.

For all the reasons stated, it is necessary to standardize procedures and frequent audits help to ensure standard procedures are receiving more than lip service.

IN CONCLUSION

All processes are the same in that they consist of equipment, raw material, people, and methods. Yet, each process is unique in terms of the variation that is inherent to a specific process. Understanding the nature of the variation that is unique to a specific process is the key to applying classic problem-solving tools that have been proven to be effective regardless of what is being manufactured, thus dispelling the myth that *our process is different.*

Problem-solving tools can be applied universally, but one size does not fit all.

REFERENCE

http://dictionary.reference.com/browse/science?s=t

5

Measurement Process Myths

The Measure of success is not whether you have a tough problem to deal with, but whether it is the same problem you had last year.

John Foster Dulles

MANAGEMENT MYTH

We need better measurement equipment.

One of the most prevalent myths in manufacturing is the mistaken belief that existing measurement devices need to be periodically replaced with devices that are advertised as having better accuracy and improved resolution when compared to the older, existing model. This particular myth is especially insidious because the selection and purchase of the wrong measurement device can have far-reaching implications with respect to the competitiveness of a manufacturing facility. And, as a practical matter the act of measuring the output of a manufacturing process is a process unto itself of which the measurement device is only a part and probably not the most important part. Finally, I would add that just like any other process, the measurement process will be affected by variation.

THE MEASUREMENT PROCESS

People

Every measurement process involves people. Different people will prepare samples to be measured using various techniques, which will contribute to measurement variation. And, the same person measuring the same sample several times will often record measurements that are not identical. Also, two different people might have very different techniques when measuring the same product characteristic, which will also result in measurement variation.

Measured Product

The physical characteristics of the item being measured will often contribute to introducing variation of measurements. Consider the measurement variation resulting from an operator taking several diameter measurements on a piece of hollow plastic tube with a micrometer. Multiple measurements taken on a machined steel component with the same micrometer would likely evidence less measurement variation.

Measurement Procedures

Measurement procedures are not nearly as common as manufacturing standard operating procedures (SOPs), and when measurement procedures do exist, they rarely offer specific directions for the selection and preparation of samples. Variation in the selection and preparation of samples can be a major contributor to measurement variation.

Measurement Equipment

The measurement equipment must be considered in terms of accuracy, resolution, precision, and discrimination. Unfortunately, manufacturers of measurement equipment only promote their equipment in terms of accuracy and resolution, and in general, manufacturers respond to the belief that better accuracy and resolution will always enhance their ability to produce higher-quality product.

Accuracy versus Precision

Accuracy

Accuracy is comparison to a known value. In manufacturing the accuracy of measurement devices is attained by means of calibration programs that are typically part of every manufacturing facility's quality control effort. In many facilities, all the micrometers, vernier calipers, dial indicators, and other handheld measurement devices are periodically collected by a quality department technician and calibrated using standards. For example, gauge blocks certified to the National Bureau of Standards are often used to calibrate micrometers and vernier calipers. If a micrometer reads 0.2505 when measuring a 0.250-gauge block, the technician typically makes adjustments until the micrometer reading agrees with the gauge block designation. After a micrometer is compared to and is in agreement with a range of different size gauge blocks, it receives a dated calibration sticker. Gram scales and other major electronic measurement devices are often calibrated by an outside agency, also with the aid of certified standards.

Periodic calibration is necessary. However, it is not in the best interest of a manufacturing facility to rely solely on calibration programs to ensure the efficacy of their measurement processes.

Once a micrometer is calibrated, people are given the task of going to the shop floor to use the micrometer, which was calibrated on a perfectly flat, incompressible, hardened steel block, to make quality and production decisions when measuring manufactured product. These decisions might be made after measuring the lengths of compressible springs, the diameters of flexible electrical connectors, the thickness of compressible rubber drive belts, the diameters of machined shafts that may not be perfectly round, and so on. There is no reason to believe that a micrometer calibrated on a gauge block will in any way reflect the true dimension of flexible, compressible, imperfectly shaped product. Calibrating a micrometer on a standard ensures accuracy when measuring the standard, but the calibration provides no assurance of the precision of measurements made with the calibrated micrometer on product produced on the shop floor.

Precision

Precision is the ability of a measurement process to repeat measurements. A micrometer is a simple measurement device until it is picked up by an individual for the purpose of making a measurement; then, the micrometer becomes part of a total measurement process. Precision refers to the ability of a measurement device, when operated by a single individual, measuring the same part multiple times in the same location, to record consistent measurements. The term *consistent measurements* is used because it is recognized that it is almost impossible for an individual to repeat any task in exactly the same way multiple times, and this is true when making multiple measurements. When the multiple measurements have a certain level of consistency, we can deem the measurement process as being stable. However, when the measurements exceed that level of required consistency, the measurement process is determined to be unstable and disqualified from measuring the specific product characteristic in question.

An imprecise (unstable) measurement process used to measure product may result in good product being scrapped and bad product being shipped to the customer.

Resolution versus Discrimination

Resolution

Resolution, when dealing with measurement equipment, refers to the smallest unit of measurement the equipment is capable of registering. Simply stated, if the resolution of a micrometer is advertised as 0.0001, that means the micrometer can record measurements in increments as low as 0.0001.

Discrimination

Discrimination is ability of a measurement process to distinguish between measured samples that were manufactured during a period of normal variation. If manufactured product is made during a stable period when the center of the bell-shaped curve is not unpredictably changing, we want the measurement process to be able to tell the difference between samples that fall within the bell-shaped curve. A valuable measurement device is one that can help us reduce normal variation and make as much product as close to the customer's nominal as possible. If the measurement device has a resolution of 0.001 and the smallest unit of variation (standard deviation) under the bell-shaped curve is 0.0005, we cannot use this measurement process to improve the process. Also, we will have an inflated estimate of the true variation of the product (see the discussion in Chapter 8 on standard deviation).

ELONGATION TESTER QUALIFICATION CASE STUDY

A major manufacturer of polymeric-coated product required shop floor personnel to test percentage elongation of the polymeric material periodically at initial process setup and several times during each shift. Elongation measurements were carefully recorded at the workstations and periodically collected and filed with quality control records. Between the shop floor, quality control, the materials laboratory, and research and development (R&D), a total of approximately eighty elongation testers were in use.

A supplier of specialized test equipment contacted the manufacturer and announced the introduction of a new elongation tester with improved resolution. Before the decision was made to expend a significant amount of money to replace the existing elongation testers with the newer model, it was strongly recommended that one new model be loaned to the manufacturer for a period of several days. During this period of time, a measurement study would be performed on the new model and compared to a measurement study performed on one of the existing elongation testers.

Over an 8-hour period, which everyone agreed was sufficient time for the process to experience normal variation, enough 12-inch long samples were chosen to support measurement studies on one existing tensile tester and one proposed newer model.

Precision or repeatability is determined by measuring the same sample more than once. And, because testing tensile strength is a destruct test (the sample is pulled apart in order to measure tensile strength), we have to be creative in testing for precision.

Each 12-inch long sample was cut in half, and because the entire length of the sample was made in a very brief span of time (extruder speeds for this type of product are typically in excess of 1,000 feet per minute), we assume the two halves of each sample essentially possess identical physical characteristics and when tested can be considered as one sample having been tested twice.

Analyzing samples taken, in this case, over an 8-hour period enable determination of the discrimination of the measurement system, and measuring the same sample twice enabled determination of the precision of the measurement system.

Both the old and the proposed new tensile testers were analyzed as briefly described. Both measurement systems were equally precise, both had the same ability to discriminate between samples made during normal variation, and both could discriminate between good and bad product.

The decision was made by management not to purchase the new equipment, and the company realized a cost avoidance of more than $150,000.

IN CONCLUSION

Companies that invent and manufacture measurement equipment advertise and promote their product in terms of accuracy and resolution. Accuracy is comparison to a known standard. For a micrometer, the known standard is a gauge block certified by the National Bureau of Standards. A micrometer may be extremely accurate when measuring the standard, but when measuring compressible molded plastic parts, it may not be at all precise. Accuracy has nothing to do with precision.

A specific measurement device may have resolution of 0.001, but if the variation of your product, in terms of standard deviation units, is on the order of 0.0005, you will not be able to discriminate between parts that are in close proximity under the bell-shaped curve, and more important, you will have an erroneous and inflated estimate of the variation of your product.

Finally, I suggest *all* existing measurement devices be qualified in terms of precision and discrimination and *never* purchase a new measurement device without qualifying it on your product first.

The bibliography offers several books that have complete discussions of the measurement process analysis.

6

Only Adjust One Process Parameter at a Time

In God we trust. All others must bring data.

W. Edwards Deming

My first job in manufacturing was as a glorified machine operator. I made molded samples for a development engineering department. I must have done something right because after only 3 months I was promoted to third-shift assistant supervisor of the molding department. This was another glorified position because my responsibilities included going from one molding machine to another for the purpose of inspecting random samples and making adjustments if I identified defects.

My instructions were quite clear. If I detected a defect, I could make an adjustment to time *or* temperature *or* pressure, then wait for some ill-defined period of time to allow the process to settle out, then take another sample. If the defect was still present, I could make a further adjustment to the parameter I had already manipulated. *Or,* if instead I chose to adjust one of the two remaining parameters that were open to me, I must return the recently adjusted parameter to its original setting.

The rule simply and clearly stated was to make only one adjustment at a time. The rationale behind the rule was as follows: If you make more than one adjustment at a time and the defect goes away, we will not know which adjustment to which process parameter made the problem go away.

SHOP FLOOR AND MANAGEMENT MYTH

When problem solving, never change more than one parameter at a time.

I regret to report that this myth is alive and well today.

As a matter of fact, within the last several months an engineer confronted me with this myth. It continues to be nourished and kept alive by the same mistaken belief that if more than one process parameter is adjusted at the same time and the problem is, in fact, solved, knowledge of which process parameter was causing the problem will not be apparent. I know this foundation of the myth to be true because these were almost the exact words used by the engineer who was attempting to persuade me not to use evolutionary optimization (EVOP) to solve a rather complex manufacturing problem.

Evolutionary optimization is a shop floor problem-solving technique that allows for making changes to two, even three, process parameters at the same time. The changes must be made in a predetermined mathematically balanced manner. I would ask the reader to accept the "mathematically balanced" comment at face value because I do not plan to go into the mathematics and statistics that justify the use of this technique (see the discussion of EVOP in Chapter 8). I discuss the nonmathematical aspects of this problem-solving tool as well as provide several case studies to demonstrate how successfully this tool can be applied to very different processes.

EVOLUTIONARY OPTIMIZATION

Adjusting one process parameter at a time may very well provide an indication of one of the process parameters that contributes to the product defect under investigation. Unfortunately, many times after it appears we have created a breakthrough because a product defect was eliminated moments after adjusting a single process parameter, the problem returns after an absence that might range from less than an hour to several days.

CATHETER TUBE EXAMPLE CASE STUDY

Some catheter tubes used in medical practices are reinforced by braiding flat wire over the base catheter tube and then, by means of a second extrusion process, providing a smooth surface over the relatively rough surface of the braided tube. A very expensive scrap problem results when the second extrusion process pushes back or displaces the flat braid wire.

An East Coast manufacturer of medical catheter tubes was plagued by braid displacement to the extent that scheduled customer deliveries were being seriously delayed. The customer became concerned enough to send one of its own engineers to the catheter tube supplier's facility in order to help solve the problem.

The engineer spent several days at the supplier facility, during which time she requested the extruder operator change a process parameter such as the line speed and then monitored the percentage scrap due to displaced braid to determine if the change in line speed solved the problem. If the problem was not solved, she would direct the operator to put the line speed back to where it was and change the unwind tension; if changing the unwind tension did not solve the problem, she directed the operator to put the unwind tension back to its previous setting and directed the operator to change … and so on.

Over the several days of the visiting engineer's change this and change that method of problem solving, the braid displacement appeared to be eliminated, at which time victory was declared, and the engineer began to plan her departure. Each time she attempted to depart, her plans were confounded because the braid displacement reappeared as many times as it appeared to go away. Eventually, the engineer departed, pointing an unsubstantiated finger at the unusually high humidity as the root cause of the braid displacement.

I find it amazing the number of times weather conditions are blamed for manufacturing process problems.

NOT UNCOMMON

There is a high probability that anyone who has ever spent time solving shop floor manufacturing problems has experienced the pain of making an adjustment that apparently solved the problem only to be informed some time later that the problem had returned. Sometimes, the problem will return even before the end of the shift, and sometimes it comes back after several days.

This situation can be painful. There is always the brief pain of the problem returning that is reflected in the problem solver's battered ego. Or, the pain can be more lasting and damaging if it is the result of the problem solver who announces, "I did fix it, so something must have changed in the process after my fix."

Let the games begin.

Meetings are scheduled. Teams are formed, which results in more meetings. Reports are generated, and the raw material comes under scrutiny; operators are closely monitored to ensure they adhere to the standard operating procedure (SOP); the SOP is reviewed; the equipment is scrutinized, and so on. Every aspect of the process is sliced, diced, examined, and vetted, but still the problem comes and goes.

CLASSES OF PROBLEMS

In manufacturing as in life, there are two classes of problems. One class of the typical manufacturing problem is referred to as sporadic problems, and the other class is chronic problems. A sporadic problem comes and goes unexpectedly; a chronic problem is one that is always with us.

Dr. Joseph M. Juran, in one of his seminars, presented a humorous anecdote that he used to describe the difference between a sporadic problem and a chronic problem. Winston Churchill, the prime minister of Great Britain during World War II, and Lady Astor, the first female member of Parliament, were political rivals and were given to witty exchanges. For example, Lady Astor once said to Mr. Churchill, "If you were my husband, sir, I would feed you poison." Mr. Churchill responded, "Madam, if I was your husband I'd drink the poison."

On one particular social engagement they both attended, the following exchange took place:

Lady Astor: Mr. Churchill, you're drunk!
Winston Churchill: Yes, I am drunk and you, madam, are ugly. But tomorrow, I shall be sober and you will still be ugly.

Dr. Juran's point was that Churchill was known for his love of liquor at social functions—he had a sporadic problem. He drank too much on occasion. If Lady Astor was ugly—she had a chronic problem. (In fact, Lady Astor was incredibly attractive, and Churchill *was* drunk.) Nevertheless, it is a humorous anecdote that is useful in that it illustrates the difference between sporadic and chronic.

In manufacturing, a chronic problem is one that we have learned to live with, perhaps because the solution is too costly or it is the result of technological limitations. The cost of a chronic problem is often passed on to the customer. Refer to the concept of allowable scrap level discussed in Chapter 3.

A sporadic problem, on the other hand, comes and goes, just like drunk and sober. It is often necessary to solve a sporadic problem due to a number of reasons. The cost of the problem may be so large it cannot be passed on to the customer; it is associated with a product characteristic that is critical to the customer's use or the like.

Finally, a sporadic problem is more difficult to solve than a chronic problem because it, literally, is not always available to work on.

The braid displacement problem experienced at the catheter tube manufacturer was definitely a sporadic problem. The question now becomes: What is the root cause of a sporadic problem? Did, in fact, the process undergo a change that cancelled out the engineer's adjustment that, for a time, eliminated the product defect? The short answer is, "Yes, the process likely did undergo a change." The long answer is, "Yes, but the change would not be recognized by many problem solvers because it was, in all probability, part of an *interaction* between two key process parameters that very likely were within the process settings specified in the SOP."

INTERACTIONS

In manufacturing, an interaction between two process parameters we will call A and B is present when the effect that process parameter A has on the product changes depending on the setting of parameter B (see Figure 6.1). In context of an example, such as the previously mentioned catheter tube displaced braid problem, let us assume, for discussion purposes only, there existed an unknown (fictional) interaction between line speed and the diameter of the braided tube.

Author's Note: Due to their very nature and the competiveness they often bring to a manufacturer once discovered, interactions are usually considered to be proprietary. Therefore, I need to emphasize in this example that the line speed/tube diameter interaction is fictional and offered only to enhance the understanding of interactions in general.

Table 6.1 provides the standard operating procedure (SOP) authorized line speeds and braided tube diameters.

Let's consider the following series of events that might have caused the visiting engineer's frustration with her attempts to solve the displaced braid problem: When the engineer arrived on the shop floor, the operators were struggling with approximately 60 percent scrap rate due to displaced braid. Her first action was to compare the process parameter settings to

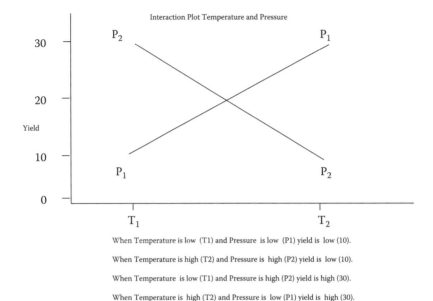

When Temperature is low (T1) and Pressure is low (P1) yield is low (10).

When Temperature is high (T2) and Pressure is high (P2) yield is low (10).

When Temperature is low (T1) and Pressure is high (P2) yield is high (30).

When Temperature is high (T2) and Pressure is low (P1) yield is high (30).

FIGURE 6.1
Interaction plot temperature and pressure.

TABLE 6.1

Standard Operating Procedure for Catheter Tube Line Speed and Braided Tube Diameter Settings

	Nominal	Low	High
Line speed (feet per minute)	1,000	800	1,200
Braided tube diameter (inches)	0.100	0.095	0.105

the SOP requirements to ensure the settings were within limits established by the SOP. Comparing process settings to the SOP is always a good idea. She noticed the line speed was at the maximum setting of 1,200 feet per minute, and she directed the operator to lower the line speed to the SOP minimum of 800 feet per minute. Figure 6.2 illustrates the results of this fictitious interaction. Specifically, when the line speed is set at 1,200 feet per minute and the braided tube diameter is 0.095 inch, the anticipated scrap level is approximately 60 percent.

The first proactive step the engineer took was to direct the operator to lower the line speed to the lowest level permitted by the SOP: 800 feet per minute. Note on Figure 6.2 that, due to the interaction, when the line speed

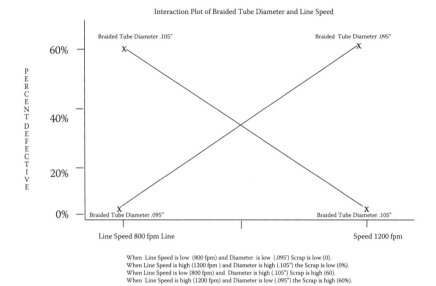

Interaction Plot of Braided Tube Diameter and Line Speed

When Line Speed is low (800 fpm) and Diameter is low (.095') Scrap is low (0).
When Line Speed is high (1200 fpm) and Diameter is high (.105") the Scrap is low (0%).
When Line Speed is low (800 fpm) and Diameter is high (.105") Scrap is high (60).
When Line Speed is high (1200 fpm) and Diameter is low (.095") the Scrap is high (60%).

FIGURE 6.2
Interaction plot of braided tube diameter and line speed.

is set at 800 feet per minute and the braided tube diameter is 0.095 inch, the scrap rate is close to zero. The visiting engineer very likely thought, "Well, that was easy!"

Of course, the engineer was unaware of the stated interaction between line speed and braided tube diameter, so she declared victory and announced the line speed must not exceed a line speed of 800 feet per minute. If the line speed exceeded 800 feet per minute, she assured everyone the displaced braid problem would be sure to come back.

This low line speed of 800 feet per minute would seriously impact the profitability of the product, but it was decided to proceed with the engineer's suggestion in view of the anticipated lower scrap rate.

And, being human, the visiting engineer might very well have formed a rather dismal opinion of the local problem-solving abilities because her solution was so simple.

Halfway through the shift, a new batch of braided tubes arrived at the extrusion station from the braiding department. Let us now assume this batch of braided tubes was manufactured at the upper diameter specification of 0.105 inch.

When this new batch of 0.105-inch diameter tubes was introduced to the final extrusion process with the line speed firmly at 800 feet per minute,

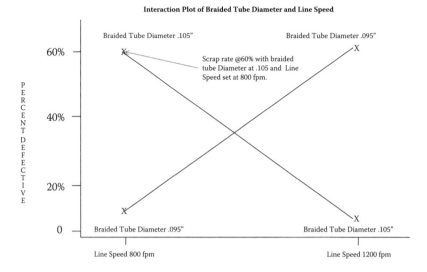

FIGURE 6.3
Interaction plot of braided tube diameter and line speed.

the scrap rate due to braid displacement jumped from close to zero to over approximately 60 percent (see Figure 6.3).

The engineer revisited the extrusion process confident the operators had increased the line speed, which would have confounded her recommended solution. She found, to her dismay, that the process was running exactly as she had suggested; the line speed was set at 800 feet per minute. She requested the operator to adjust the line speed back to the original 1,200 feet per minute, and the scrap rate was reduced to the very desirable level of close to zero.

Her conclusion therefore was the line speed was not, as she originally concluded, a key factor in controlling braid displacement scrap. Something else in the process must have changed in coincidence with her reduction of line speed to 800 feet per minute that produced a remarkable, but temporary, reduction in scrap due to braid displacement.

She decided to leave the line speed at 1,200 feet per minute while she had the screw speed changed from its present setting at nominal. First, she increased the screw speed slightly, then she decreased the screw speed slightly with no change to the low scrap level.

Screw speed was set back at nominal, and she made slight adjustments to rewind tension and detected no significant change in braid displacement scrap. Rewind tension was reset to where it was, and unwind tension was the next subject of experimental change.

This method of adjusting one process parameter at a time for the balance of the day and all of the next day resulted in no conclusions regarding the root cause of braid displacement.

With the line speed set at 1,200 feet per minute, the low level of scrap would continue until a lot of braided tubes that were at or close to the 0.095-inch diameter was introduced, which would cause the scrap rate to soar to the high level for no apparent reason.

But, in the absence of understanding the concept of interactions, the engineer's attention would turn to exploring other aspects of the process.

She might first turn to the raw material and review the certificates of conformance (COCs) received with each batch of polymer and determine that the melt index, modulus of elongation, tensile, and so on of each batch was, on the average, within required specifications; therefore, she would likely decide the problem of braid displacement could not be the result of the polymer.

A myth regarding COCs is discussed in Chapter 7.

Her attention might then turn to the COC for the braid wire, which was also in order.

Perhaps she would then perform dimensional inspection on several incoming lots of braid wire and find the width and thickness dimensions to be within the specifications provided to the braid wire supplier.

Then, she might perform dimensional inspection on several batches of braided tubes produced over a period of several shifts by the braiding department. She would find all the samples of braided tubes to be within specification. Her conclusion would logically be the problem of braid displacement scrap could not be due to the braided tubes because they were all within specification.

Please note the engineer found all the raw material used by the second extrusion process, *including the braided tubes*, to be within specification; therefore, her decision would, in all probability, be the root cause of braid displacement could not be due to the raw material.

This brings us to a shop floor myth closely related to problem solving in general.

SHOP FLOOR AND MANAGEMENT MYTH

As long as component parts of a process are within specification, they cannot possibly be contributing to product defects.

This newest myth is discussed in detail in Chapter 7.

To emphasize a critical point of our scenario, all raw materials were deemed to be within specification; therefore, raw material could not possibly be contributing to the problem of braid displacement.

This conclusion is wrong on several levels. Please refer to the discussion in Chapter 2 on how specifications are often derived.

I know I am repeating myself, but convincing people to break away from what I refer to as the "specification mentality" often requires repetition.

Beyond the inappropriate methods used to determine specifications discussed in Chapter 2, the engineer, during her problem-solving journey to identify the root cause of braid displacement, was totally ignoring the possibility of an interaction between two or more process parameters that might be affecting the scrap rate.

In this case, we are pretending the line speed and braided tube diameter were interacting as illustrated in Figure 6.2.

Let us review the interaction.

- When the line speed is set at the SOP low level of 800 feet per minute and the diameter of the braided tubes just by chance happens to be at the minimum SOP diameter of 0.095 inch, the scrap due to braid displacement was close to zero.
- When the line speed is set high at 1,200 feet per minute and the diameter of the braided tubes happens to be at the maximum SOP diameter of 1.05 inch, the scrap due to braid displacement is also close to zero.
- When the line speed is set low at 800 feet per minute and diameter of the braided tubes happens to be at the maximum SOP diameter of 1.05 inch, the scrap due to braid displacement is close to 60 percent.
- When the line speed is set high at 1,200 feet per minute and diameter of the braided tubes happens to be at the minimum SOP diameter of 0.095 inch, the scrap due to braid displacement is close to 60 percent.

Why did the lot of braided tubes being processed when the engineer had the line speed reduced to 800 feet per minute, and saw the braid displacement plummet to zero, have a diameter of 0.095 inch?

In all probability, the operator who produced this lot of extruded tubes that went to the braiding department liked to run the tube diameter on the low end of the specification, 0.095 inch. When these low-diameter tubes produced at 0.095 inch were combined with a line speed of 1,200 feet per minute, the scrap was approximately 60 percent.

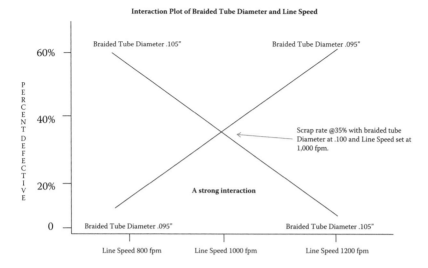

FIGURE 6.4
Interaction plot of braided tube diameter and line speed.

When the engineer directed the line speed to be lowered to 800 feet per minute, the scrap rate dropped to almost zero. Therefore, absent knowledge of the concept of interactions, the engineer believed her solution to be valid.

Why did the next batch of tubes introduced to the final extrusion process have a diameter of 0.105 inch, resulting in the braid displacement scrap jumping up to 60 percent? It is very likely the operator who produced these tubes liked to run on the high side of diameter. When this batch of braided tubes produced with the tube diameter at 0.105 inch was introduced to the process and the line speed remained unchanged at 800 feet per minute, the scrap rate jumped to 60 percent (see Figure 6.4).

The engineer in this example was being confounded by an unknown interaction. She had fallen prey to the myth: *When problem solving never change more than one parameter at a time.*

My fervent hope is that by now the reader will understand the need, when problem solving, to test for interactions.

I am paraphrasing Doctor W. Edwards Deming when I say: Any critical product characteristic is dependent on two or three *key* process parameters. I would add to this observation the fact that the two or three key process parameters often interact.

Understanding and accepting the concept that an interaction between two or more process parameters is a fact of manufacturing is, in my experience, 75 percent of the challenge. The challenge is to introduce to management and shop floor associates a simplified EVOP method for the purpose of enabling shop floor personnel to efficiently and factually solve shop floor problems.

THE PROBLEM-SOLVING MATRIX

If the engineer in the catheter tube example had been knowledgeable in the area of interactions, she might have capitalized on her inclination that line speed was a key process parameter in determining the amount of braid displacement defects.

It is also desirable to acknowledge the prime directive while problem solving: do not interfere with production. In rare circumstances, this is not possible—the operative word being *rare*.

To begin, the engineer might choose to investigate an interaction between line speed and barrel temperature (see Table 6.2). Table 6.2 represents the most basic form of the classic problem-solving matrix. With two process parameters and using the two levels of maximum and minimum settings prescribed in the SOP, there are only four possible combinations of maximum/minimum levels that can be trialed. And, if we construct the matrix in such a way that we do not exceed the levels of the SOP, we have an expectation of not interfering with production while attempting to solve the braid displacement problem. This is a good thing.

It would be prudent to select twenty five samples at random during a 15-minute run with the line speed and barrel temperature set according to run 1 (line speed = 1,200 fpm/barrel temperature = 410°F) and list the percentage defective due to braid displacement found in the random sample

TABLE 6.2

Two-Parameter, Two-Level Experimental Matrix

Run	Factor A Line Speed	Factor B Barrel Temperature	Response Percentage Braid Displacement
1	+ (1,200 fpm)	+ (410°F)	57
2	+ (1,200 fpm)	– (390°F)	62
3	– (800 fpm)	– (390°F)	49
4	– (800 fpm)	+ (410°F)	59

in the response column; in this example, 57 percent of the sample demonstrated braid displacement.

The percentage defective for runs 2, 3, and 4 are listed in their respective response column in Table 6.2.

Within the range of line speed and barrel temperature SOP requirements, any reasonable and prudent person would conclude, based on the four responses, that no interaction exists between line speed and barrel temperature regarding the increase or decrease of percentage defective due to braid displacement.

Taking this procedure a step further, let us assume the engineer was a reasonable and prudent individual and discounted a line speed/barrel temperature interaction as it related to braid displacement and decided to perform a similar trial with line speed and braided tube diameter (see Table 6.3). The results in the response column of Table 6.3 speak to the fact there is a significant interaction between line speed and braided tube diameter.

Volumes have been written regarding the statistical significance of experimental results. Nothing beats replication. Repeat the results and be confident in announcing the problem has been solved. The objection to this procedure is often stated in terms of "What if you choose the wrong two parameters to trial?" If you choose the "wrong two parameters" and you obtain results as in Table 6.2, we can now discount those two process parameters as not interacting.

And, we are not limited to a two-process-parameter/two-level matrix. Table 6.4 offers a three-process parameter/two-level matrix.

There are other matrices that cover seven process parameters and more, but these are more complex and do not fall within the purview of this book.

I suggest for shop floor problem solving a three-process parameter/two-level matrix is about as complicated you need for most occasions.

TABLE 6.3

Two-Factor, Two-Level Experimental Matrix

Run	Factor A Line Speed	Factor B Tube Diameter (inches)	Response Percentage Braid Displacement
1	+ (1,200 fpm)	+ (0.105)	3
2	+ (1,200 fpm)	– (0.095)	57
3	– (800 fpm)	– (0.095)	4
4	– (800 fpm)	+ (0.105)	61

TABLE 6.4

Three-Factor, Two-Level Experimental Matrix

Run	Material Thickness	Air Pressure	Speed	Response
1	+	+	+	
2	+	+	−	
3	+	−	-	
4	+	−	+	
5	−	-	−	
6	−	-	+	
7	−	+	+	
8	−	+	−	

THE INTERACTION PLOT

In the following case study, I demonstrate, using only addition, how to construct interaction plots as illustrated in Figure 6.1. The manner in which the two lines on Figure 6.1 cross in the center indicate a strong interaction between the two process parameters. Figure 6.5 illustrates two process parameters that do not interact.

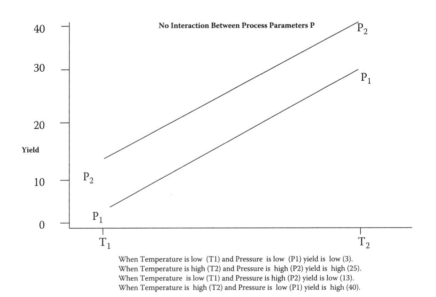

When Temperature is low (T1) and Pressure is low (P1) yield is low (3).
When Temperature is high (T2) and Pressure is high (P2) yield is high (25).
When Temperature is low (T1) and Pressure is high (P2) yield is low (13).
When Temperature is high (T2) and Pressure is low (P1) yield is high (40).

FIGURE 6.5
No interaction between process parameters P.

MISSING PARTS CASE STUDY

A Canadian manufacturer of telecommunication components was experiencing a serious problem of missing components that were prepackaged and shipped with telecommunication equipment.

Any parent assembling toys on Christmas Eve who has come up short one bolt or two specialized clips needed to assemble a toy can understand the frustration of a field engineer, at the top of a communication tower, missing one prepackaged component needed to finish an installation.

The packaging engineers had been making modifications to the automatic packaging line for months without solving the problem of missing parts. They had identified the following process parameters that were considered to be critical to the problem of missing clips.

- Packaging line
- Air pressure
- Speed of conveyor system
- Bowl design
- Type of package

The problem was further defined by plotting historical percentage of missing parts data. It was determined that the defect called "missing parts" was discovered in approximately 8 percent of samples selected at random from the output of the several packaging lines. On occasion, the defect rate would jump to 11 percent, and conversely, some random samples proved to have zero missing parts.

A number of attempts had been made to identify the root cause of missing parts.

One effort was directed at air pressure on station A1. The air pressure was set according to the SOP nominal requirement, and during the next hour a forty-piece sample of filled packages was selected and checked for missing parts. The random sample of forty packages contained four packages with missing parts for a 10 percent defect rate. Then, the air pressure was set at several pounds per square inch (psi) units above the SOP upper limit, and the random sample selected over the next hour indicated a defect rate of 14 percent. This was interpreted as the air pressure having been adjusted in the wrong direction. At this point in time, the air pressure was decreased to 1 psi below the SOP lower limit. The forty-piece random sample contained only 2 percent defective packages due to missing parts. Unfortunately, the 2 percent success was short lived, and several hours later the missing parts problem came back without warning.

The problem solvers decided to adjust the speed of the conveyor line in the same way they adjusted the air pressure. This effort produced no positive results.

This is another classic case of ignoring the possibility of interactions taking place.

After several weeks of narrowly focused attempts at identifying the root cause of the missing parts by adjusting this and trying that, not only was

TABLE 6.5

Three-Process-Parameter, Two-Level Problem-Solving Matrix

Run	Air Pressure	Conveyor Speed	Type of Package	Response Percentage Defective
1	+	+	+	2.8
2	+	+	–	6.2
3	+	–	–	2.0
4	+	–	+	4.2
5	–	–	–	0.7
6	–	–	+	2.5
7	–	+	+	7.0
8	–	+	–	7.7

the group discouraged but also no one could accurately remember what had been tried as opposed to what had not been tried.

The group was encouraged to use a three-process-parameter/two-level problem-solving matrix. At the very least, employing the matrix technique provides a record of exactly what conditions have been trialed as well as a factual record of the results.

The three process parameters chosen were air pressure, conveyor speed, and type of package. Once again, out of concern for the proprietary nature of the end discovery, these were not the actual parameters chosen by the group. I offer them only for demonstration purposes (see Table 6.5). Notice this matrix calls for a total of eight combinations as opposed to the two-process-parameter/two-level matrix. This is because with three process parameters trialed there are a total of eight possible combinations of plus and minus levels.

Some interesting mathematics would be employed by some people to analyze the results in the response column. I suggest most people would prefer to forgo the statistical voodoo and rank the plus and minus combinations in ascending order of the results found in the response column (see Table 6.6).

Comparing the combinations of pluses and minuses to the values in the response column does not reveal any apparent pattern. This is a fairly reliable, nonmathematical, method that gives us a tentative indication that no one process parameter is dominant.

Testing for interaction by means of creating an interaction plot involves a little bit of adding and dividing. Please note in Table 6.6 the responses are in descending order, and the responses are lined up with the combinations of pluses and minuses that created those responses.

In this table, air pressure and type of package rows 1 and 8 each have two combinations of minus, minus (– –) that contributed to creating the responses of 0.7 and 7.7, respectively. Rows 2 and 6 each have two combinations of plus, minus (+ –) that contributed to creating responses of 2.0 and

TABLE 6.6

Three-Process-Parameter, Two-Level Problem-Solving Matrix

Run	Air Pressure	Conveyor Speed	Type of Package A(−); B(+)	Response (Percentage)
1	−	−	−	0.7
2	+	−	−	2.0
3	−	−	+	2.5
4	+	+	+	2.8
5	+	−	+	4.2
6	+	+	−	6.2
7	−	+	+	7.0
8	−	+	−	7.7

6.2, respectively. Rows 3 and 7 have two combinations of minus, plus (− +) that contributed to creating responses of 2.5 and 7.0, respectively. Rows 4 and 5 have two combinations of plus, plus (+ +) that contributed to creating responses of 2.8 and 4.2, respectively.

The average response of each pair of combinations is determined as follows:

Rows 1 and 8, − −	0.70 + 7.7 = 8.4/2 = 4.20
Rows 2 and 6, + −	2.0 + 6.2 = 8.2/2 = 4.10
Rows 3 and 7, − +	2.5 + 7.0 = 9.5/2 = 4.75
Rows 4 and 5, + +	2.8 + 4.2 = 7.0/2 = 3.50

Using the averages of 4.2, 4.1, 4.75, and 3.5, we can construct the interaction plot illustrated in Table 6.7.

Note that varying the air pressure from the upper limit to the lower limit of the SOP requirement while we trial both types of packages does not change the average responses much. Figure 6.6 is a good illustration of a weak interaction. This is also a good example demonstrating the first matrix that is trialed does not always provide the answer sought.

TABLE 6.7

Plotting an Interaction

	Type of Package	Air Pressure	Average of Two Runs with Identical Signs
7.7 + 0.70 = 8.4/12 = 4.20	−	−	4.2
2.0 + 6.2 = 8.2/2 = 4.10	+	−	4.1
2.5 + 7.0 = 9.5/2 = 4.75	−	+	4.75
2.8 + 4.2 = 7.0/2 = 3.5	+	− +	3.5

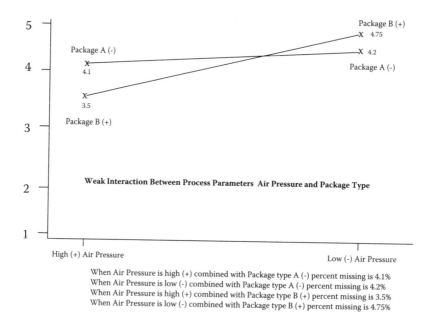

When Air Pressure is high (+) combined with Package type A (-) percent missing is 4.1%
When Air Pressure is low (-) combined with Package type A (-) percent missing is 4.2%
When Air Pressure is high (+) combined with Package type B (+) percent missing is 3.5%
When Air Pressure is low (-) combined with Package type B (+) percent missing is 4.75%

FIGURE 6.6
Weak interaction between process parameters air pressure and package type.

The reader should recognize that an important aspect of utilizing problem-solving matrices is identifying those process parameters that do not have an effect on the product characteristic under investigation, and that knowledge can provide significant benefits.

IN CONCLUSION

There are no guarantees in life, only probabilities. Experience indicates the probability is not very high that the root cause of any process problem can be identified by making adjustments to a single process parameter.

The basic problem-solving matrix will provide clues regarding what process parameters are not significant to a specific manufacturing problem, and it will clearly show any interactions that might be present.

The only difficult aspect of utilizing the problem-solving matrix is convincing others that it will work, not to mention the task of convincing others of the veracity of the results.

7

Raw Material Myths

If you don't know how to ask the right questions, you discover nothing.

W. Edwards Deming

As previously discussed, a manufacturing process consists of equipment, raw material, people, and methods (see Figure 7.1). Experience indicates that when there is a process problem causing a product defect, the first of the four components of any manufacturing process to receive attention is usually the equipment. And, the attention given to the equipment is generally in the form of making adjustments to favorite process parameters. Due to a number of the myths and bad practices discussed in previous chapters, a marathon of adjusting for several days is not uncommon in some facilities.

At some point in the process of solving a process problem, someone begins to question the raw material, and the person often runs headlong into one or more of the most common manufacturing myths that relate directly or indirectly to raw material. Raw material can be barrels of pelletized polymers, gaylords of chemicals, cans of process aids such as lubricants, mechanical components for assembly, brass bars for machining, and more. All raw materials have one thing in common: They are always purchased to certain customer-imposed specifications.

Often, when an undisciplined problem-solving exercise reaches the stage of questioning the raw material, the first action involves ensuring the raw material is to specification. If the raw material in question is found to be within specification, it is most often discounted as contributing to the product defect under investigation because of a myth that is widespread throughout manufacturing.

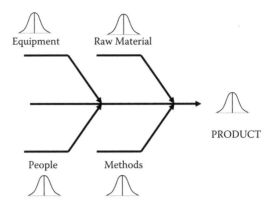

FIGURE 7.1
Process variation causes product variation.

Shop Floor and Management Manufacturing Myth

The problem cannot be the raw material; we checked it out, and it is within specification.

At times, being within specification is not the be-all and end-all that many people believe it to be.

SQUEAKY HINGE CASE STUDY

A manufacturer of telecommunication components dedicated one injection-molding line to manufacturing polymeric hinge assemblies; each hinge assembly consisted of two individual components. One of the components was designed to be affixed to the frame of a telecommunication cabinet, and the other component of the assembly was designed to be affixed to the door of the same cabinet.

The component of the hinge assembly that was mounted on the door of the cabinet consisted of a cylindrical member with a specified outer diameter of 0.299 – 0.002/+0.000 inch (0.297 to 0.299 inch). This part of the hinge assembly was designed to mate with its counterpart mounted on the frame of the cabinet; the receiving hole in the cabinet frame component of the hinge was configured with an inner diameter of 0.301 – 0.000/+0.002 inch (0.301 to 0.303 inch).

There was a chronic complaint originating from the customer's field engineers regarding the number of times they assembled the cabinets at a client location only to discover that some of the hinges, when assembled, made a high-pitched squeaking noise when the cabinet door was opened or closed. This did not happen very often but often enough to have resulted in a number of callbacks from the end users to replace the noisy hinges with hinges that did not squeak.

An analysis of one hundred samples of each component selected from the injection molding line revealed, when assembled, two of the one hundred assemblies squeaked. The two squeaking assemblies and a number of retuned hinge assemblies were examined by inspectors looking for rough surface finish, contamination, voids, dirt, excessive flash, and so on, but nothing even remotely discrepant was discovered. Also, the outer diameter of the pins and the inner diameter of the mating surfaces were measured, and all were determined to be within specification.

The investigations failed to link any of the suspected product characteristics to be the root cause of the squeaking. The squeaking hinges appeared to be identical to the nonsqueaking hinges.

The suggestion was made to select a random sample of fifty pairs of hinge components and to measure the outer diameter and the inner diameter of the two mating surfaces. The suggestion was, at first, rejected based on the fact that random samples had already been measured, and all had been deemed to be within specification. It was gently pointed out that although the previously measured samples had all been within specification, the distribution of the outer and inner diameters had not been recorded and analyzed.

A simple histogram constructed with measured data can often reveal a clue that might not be apparent by simply observing that all the data is within specification. And, it sometimes only requires one clue based on data that will lead to the root cause of a problem.

With some grumbling on the part of the inspectors (inner diameters are never fun to measure), the samples were measured and plotted in histogram form. The shaft diameters and sectioned pieces of the receiving inner diameter were measured using a precise machinist microscope (see Figure 7.2). Please note the histograms indicate that both dimensions are consuming the entire allowable specification.

Author's Note: I can assure the reader that if a basic statistical technique, which I wish to refrain from dealing with in this book, were to be applied to the histogram data, we would discover the actual distribution of the diameters would be somewhat wider than indicated by the histograms.

The significant fact with respect to this case study is the two distributions, at the very least, are taking up the entire range of inner and outer diameter specifications. This is never a good sign.

The inspectors were asked to choose pairs of components with pin diameters on the very high end and receptacle diameters on the very low end of their respective diameters. When a single part with the outer pin diameter at the very high end of the specification was selected and mated with a receptacle part with the receiving hole at the very low end of the inner diameter, the completed assembly squeaked.

Inspectors were given the task of seeking high-end outer-diameter parts and mating them with low-end inner-diameter parts. Over 80 percent of these assemblies squeaked. The cry went up: "How can this be? The assembled parts fail even though the diameters are within specification!"

A situation such as the hinge assembly under discussion "can be" due to the fact that specifications, especially with respect to mating surfaces, are often not correctly structured, specifically, little or no consideration

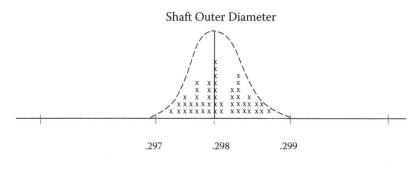

Shaft Outer Diameter

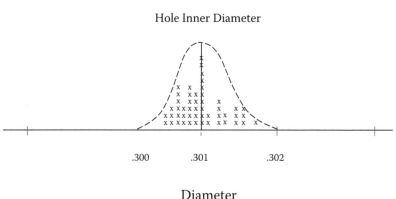

Hole Inner Diameter

Diameter

FIGURE 7.2
Molded hinge component histograms.

was given regarding how parts produced at the extreme ends of the specification range will perform. But, more important, it is not widely accepted practice in manufacturing to strive to manufacture "well within" the agreed-on specification.

If product is consuming the entire specification, the most minor shift in the output will cause some product to be produced over high specification or under low specification depending on the direction of the shift.

If the product was consuming only 75 percent of the allowable specification, then minor process average shift would not cause off-specification product to be produced.

A simple arithmetic exercise can be used to determine valid specifications based on the standard deviations of the distributions. See the discussion of process capability studies in Chapter 8.

PAPER DRIVE FEED ROLLER CASE STUDY

A New England-based corporation supplied brand-name manufacturers of office equipment with paper drive feed components for printers, copiers, fax machines, and the like. This New England manufacturer purchased raw materials, such as various polymers and hardware, including metal shafts, to which they added value and provided the end user with fully assembled and functional paper drive feed components.

One brand-name company that made and sold computers, printers, and fax machines was in the process of introducing to the market a less-expensive printer it believed would compete with foreign-made printers in quality and price. The printer manufacturer had contracted the New England-based company to provide a critical paper drive feed roller for its newly designed printer.

In order to reduce the cost of manufacturing by taking advantage of volume discounts from suppliers of component parts, the printer manufacturer decided to design similar component parts to make them multifunctional. For instance, if an economical design change could be made to a handful of similar plastic parts to make each part, when installed, perform a designated function, the manufacturer of the printers could benefit from having the cost of one mold as opposed to the cost of several molds, which theoretically would reduce the price per part. There would also be a volume discount that would not apply if many different parts were being produced instead of one "universal" part. This concept was applied to the entire printer, including the need for seven stainless steel shafts.

The printer manufacturer had contracted a Florida company to supply it with six of the seven stainless steel shafts that were directly installed in the printer without value being added to the shafts. The seventh shaft, to be provided by the New England-based manufacturer, was to have four polyurethane feed rollers adhered to the shaft, which when installed in the printer functioned as the paper drive feed roll. Moving paper in a straight path through a machine while the paper is being exposed to excessive temperatures, pressures, and tensions is not an easy task and requires highly engineered shafts and feed rolls.

The New England manufacturer awarded the contract to produce the paper drive feed rollers was strongly advised by the printer manufacturer to consider purchasing the stainless steel shafts that it would require from the Florida-based manufacturer. In this way, the New England manufacturer would benefit from the volume discount as well. Obviously, the intent of the printer manufacturer in making this suggestion was to avoid the unnecessary expense the paper drive feed roller supplier would incur in dealing with a second shaft manufacturer, thus minimizing the cost to the printer manufacturer of the paper drive feed rolls. This suggestion made good business sense and was readily accepted by the paper drive feed roller manufacturer.

In keeping with the standard operating procedure for qualifying new suppliers, the paper drive feed roller manufacturer initiated a purchase order for a sample quantity of 1,000 shafts from the Florida manufacturer. When the sample shipment was received, an inspector was dispatched to the warehouse to select a fifty-piece random sample that would receive a "first-off" inspection of all nonreference blueprint dimensions.

The inspection procedures at the New England facility were in the process of transitioning from the World War II era Military Standard 105 attribute inspection plan to a more informative, more efficient, statistically

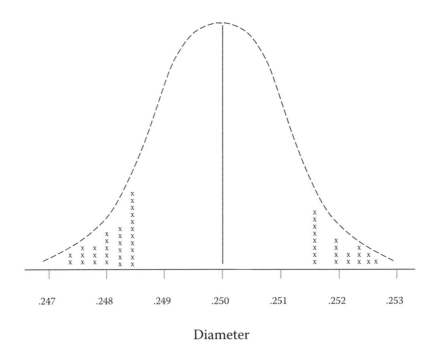

FIGURE 7.3

Shaft-bearing surface histogram.

based, inspection procedure. The first step in this transition was to have all measurements for incoming hardware recorded on a histogram.

The inspector, contrary to his normal demeanor, was grinning widely when he brought the half dozen shaft dimension histograms to the quality manager. A glance at the histogram representing the fifty measurements recorded for shaft bearing surface, which was the most critical dimension of the entire shaft, more than explained the inspector's smile (see Figure 7.3). The dotted line in Figure 7.3 represents an approximation of the shape the fifty measurements of the shaft bearing surface should have looked like with respect to the nominal plus and minus 0.003-inch specification.

The distribution of the *x*s represents the fifty measurements as recorded on the histogram by the inspector. What had been obvious to the inspector, ergo the wide grin, was that the shaft supplier was sorting out the best parts, which would be shipped to the large printer manufacturer, and sending the relatively small New England supplier the tail ends of the distribution.

The megasize printer manufacturer was getting the best parts, and the small roller manufacturer was getting only the highest and lowest parts with respect to the bearing surface. Sending the roller manufacturer only the highest and lowest parts could only be the result of 100 percent inspection.

Why would the shaft supplier go to the time, trouble, and expense of 100 percent sorting the production output in order to send the printer company the best shafts?

I ask the reader to remember, as previously discussed, many companies are requiring suppliers to provide product with the critical characteristics well within the upper and lower specifications. And, *well within* is described as the measurement distribution of critical characteristics must be equal to or less than 75 percent of the total specification. In all probability, the shaft supplier had been qualified by the printer manufacturer only after the supplier had sorted out any shafts that exceeded 75 percent of the bearing surface plus and minus 0.003-inch specification.

Once qualified, the shaft supplier had to continue the charade by 100 percent sorting. Then, along came the opportunity to unload all of the sorted parts on the unsuspecting roller manufacturer. As it happened, the roller manufacturer was not so unsuspecting.

In addition to being unethical, immoral, and perhaps even a little illegal, the shaft supplier's action was wrong on several other levels.

- One hundred percent inspection is not 100 percent effective. Eventually, the printer company would have received shafts from the Florida facility with out-of-specification bearing surfaces.
- It is almost certain the roller manufacturer would have received a significant number of shafts with out-of-specification bearing surfaces.
- If the tolerances of the shaft bearing surface and the mating surface in the printer were not properly calculated, as for the squeaking hinge, there would likely be early field failures of paper drive feed rollers due to the fact that approximately half of what the paper drive feed roll manufacturer would be providing the printer manufacturer would be on the high side of the specification. This would likely have resulted in customer dissatisfaction and possible warranty claims against the printer company.
- The printer company would in all probability charge back expenses to the paper drive feed roll manufacturer.
- The paper drive feed roll manufacturer would incur the expense of solving the problem imposed by the raw material.

Fortunately, a simple histogram found the raw material problem in spite of all the samples being within specification. As a result, this story had a successful conclusion for the printer company and the feed roll manufacturer. The shaft supplier did not experience a happy ending, however.

MELT INDEX CASE STUDY

The chief executive officer (CEO) of a manufacturing company that consumed a great deal of low-density polyethylene (LDPE) suspected that excessive variation of the polyethylene characteristic "melt index" might be causing his organization to experience processing problems resulting in unwanted variation in finished product. Melt index is a common measurement and provides an indication of how easily melted polymer will flow and, for instance, how consistently the polymer will interface with the material to which it is adhered.

At the request of the CEO, internal records were reviewed, and it was reported that the certificates of analysis (COAs) from the supplier of the polyethylene indicated that the melt index requirement of ten was met on every past lot received. It seemed odd to the CEO, and rightly so, that there was no variation in the melt index as it was recorded on several years' worth of COAs.

The supplier of the polyethylene, a very large company whose name would be recognized in virtually every household in the country, was contacted, and a visit by one of their field engineers was arranged. The meeting with the field engineer from the chemical supplier was enlightening. She explained that each shipment of polyethylene delivered by railroad tank car to a siding at the manufacturer's facility consisted of 240,000 pounds. The 240,000 pounds was comprised of four separate batches of material, each batch consisting of approximately 60,000 pounds. Before shipment, one sample was selected from each of the four batches and measured in order to record a melt index reading (other characteristics were also measured and recorded). The four melt index readings were averaged, and the average melt index recorded on the COA.

The question asked by the CEO at this juncture was simply, "So, if the melt indices of two batches are recorded to be eight and the melt indices of the other two batches are recorded to be twelve, the COA would indicate a melt index of … ." The chemical company representative finished the question with, "The COA would indicate a melt index of ten."

Therefore, in actuality the end user of the polyethylene did not have a true understanding of the melt index of any one single charge of material being processed during a specific period of time or any idea how much variation to expect in a particular shipment.

Just because raw material is within specification does not mean it is not contributing to process problems at the end-user's facility. And, just because the average of a data set is within specification does not, in any way, infer all the data points that contributed to the average are within specification.

DISPELLING THE MYTH

This is an easy myth to dispel. It is just a matter of requiring the supplier of raw material to provide the data used to collect the average value reported on the certificate. The data, once received by the customer, can be placed into a histogram, which will be somewhat more informative than the single average data point. Perhaps someday, this data can be used by the customer to calculate the standard deviation of the characteristic being certified, which would be even more informative than the histogram alone.

In my experience, the most damaging manufacturing myth related to raw materials involves the fact that many times suppliers of raw material change their processes without notifying their customers.

MANAGEMENT MYTH

The raw material we received today was manufactured according to the same standards as the raw material we initially approved.

FUEL DISTRIBUTION COMPONENT CASE STUDY

Beginning in the 1960s, and continuing for more than 20 years, one particular company was the sole source supplier to the automotive industry of a critical component integral to the fuel distribution system. This supplier to the automotive industry had developed a proprietary process but had never applied for a patent. Applying for a patent requires detailed disclosure of the discovery; such disclosure can enable others to slightly modify the discovery and apply for their own patent. In essence, someone can duplicate the patented discovery with a slight change, apply for his or her own patent, and become a competitor. This is why there are patent attorneys.

In not applying for a patent, the subject company could keep its secret proprietary discovery, and for over 20 years, no other company was successful in duplicating the original process. This is not to say the automotive industry did not try very hard to secure a second source as no company wishes to have a single source of critical supplied components. By the time a second source was identified, fuel distribution in automobiles had undergone great changes, and the critical component became obsolete.

But I digress.

In the mid-1970s, catastrophe struck the company that was providing this very critical component to the automotive industry. The catastrophe came in the form of a significant rise in scrap that made the majority of the product destined for the Big Three (Ford, GM, and Chrysler) useless. The scrap rose precipitously across the entire product line that consisted of numerous shapes, sizes, compound formulations, colors, and so on for no apparent reason. There did not seem to be a single common potential cause for the drastic change to the collective output.

The urgency of the problem was first addressed for a full three shifts by supervisors, inspectors, and operators on the shop floor, with the usual methods of adjusting equipment parameters to no avail. Then, engineering stepped in and tried manipulating various combinations of equipment parameters without success.

The next subject of engineering focus became the material used to manufacture the components. This very proprietary material that went into the manufacture of the many different parts provided to the customers was created on site and consisted of different blends of commercially available compounds and chemicals.

Samples of all formulations of the blended materials were submitted to the research and development laboratory for tests of tensile elongation, density, and so on. Of course, COAs of raw material components were also reviewed.

Suppliers were contacted for their expertise, and several suppliers dispatched field representatives to assist on site.

The mystery went unsolved for more than a week, and the 2-week inventory of finished goods required by contract was being worked down very rapidly.

A high-level meeting was held that included upper management, supplier representatives, scientists, engineers, production management, and supervision. The problem was reviewed, and possible root causes were offered, reviewed, and rejected.

One chemical that was common to all formulations had been reviewed and discussed prior to this meeting but had been discounted because it was a "filler" that enhanced the processability of the material. This filler was considered to be inert and did not contribute to any chemical reactions.

In desperation, the supplier of this material was contacted and interviewed by telephone. The inevitable question was posed to the supplier: "Has anything recently changed in your process?" The answer was, "No."

To make a short story even shorter, a visit to the supplier of the suspect material proved otherwise. Records indicated a change had in fact been made to the process that produced the filler. When this was pointed out, the supplier of the chemical responded, "But that minor change would not affect your process!"

The change was reversed. New material was delivered, received, and introduced to the process; the problem evaporated as quickly as it had appeared.

All too often, suppliers change their processes in the belief the change will not affect their customer's process. However, all too often the supplier knows little or nothing about its customer's process.

Sometimes, the change a supplier makes is as mundane as purchasing a less-expensive raw material from *its* supplier. Or, the change could involve the supplier purchasing its raw material from a different company in a different country that has a different standard. The change might involve the introduction of a new piece of equipment or a different method of measuring critical characteristics.

THREAD DIE COLOR CHANGE CASE STUDY

A company located in South Carolina provided components to the textile industry engaged in manufacturing fabric. Fabric manufacturing, of course, requires individual threads to be processed through looms. Modern fabric production is automated, and the threads are processed to and through the looms at very high speeds.

Various gauges of threads are processed to their end point through polymeric thread guides, which, due to the high speeds involved, are highly engineered in terms of dimensions and other physical characteristics.

A problem similar to the problem in the previous case study was experienced at the fabric manufacturer. It was similar in terms of the suddenness with which it appeared and in the inconvenience it caused the fabric manufacturer. For no apparent reason, thread began breaking throughout the fabric manufacturing facility.

This particular catastrophe only lasted for a day before the root cause was easily identified as it was obvious to management that the supplier's process had in fact changed. It was obvious because the color of the thread guides had changed from green to orange. When the situation was reported to the producer of the thread guides along with the demand the original color be reinstated, the response from the supplier was one of skepticism: "How could changing the color cause the threads to break?"

However, if the customer wants green then we will give the customer green. Shipments of green thread guides were delivered, received, installed, and the breaking thread problem evaporated as quickly as it appeared.

To the supplier's credit, it performed extensive tests on the green and orange thread guides, and it discovered the orange pigment had a very different coefficient of friction than the green pigment, which was considered the reason for the very different results when the orange thread guides were introduced.

This is another example of when a supplier of product to a customer made a minor change in its process fully believing the change would not have any effect on its customer's process, but it did. Obviously, the color change did have an effect, seriously impacting the user's process. Fortunately, the problem only lasted for a brief period of time, but an expensive period of time nevertheless.

Dispelling This Myth

This myth can be dispelled only by means of the customer being proactive. Every purchase order for raw material must include the requirement there be no changes, however minor, to the supplier's process, from the standard operating procedures, work instructions, formulations, or sources of raw material without first advising the customer of the supplier's intent. Also, periodic audits should be conducted that address the supplier's standard operating procedures, work instructions, formulations, and sources of raw material to ensure there have been no changes introduced to the process.

Finally, it must be made clear that it is incumbent on the customer's supplier that it is responsible for not to change *its* processes and the like.

Another myth that I find prevalent in manufacturing is the idea that important decisions can be made based on averaged data.

MANAGEMENT MYTH

It is safe to make decisions based on the averages of collected measurements.

I have a suspicion this myth originates, to some degree, as a result of management's willingness to accept the averaged data recorded on COAs as representative of the quality of the entire shipment.

It is common in industry to periodically engage engineering departments in the task of improving processes by modifying or replacing major pieces of equipment, changing raw material suppliers, or revising standard operating procedures. All of these activities should involve a factual data-based evaluation of the process before, as well as after, the process has been revised.

Unfortunately, the culture in some manufacturing facilities does not rely heavily on data to make expensive decisions but rather allows decisions to be made based on internal opinions, studies provided by sales representatives, or past experiences of senior members of the organization.

I have seldom seen data-based studies included in capital requests. I have seen studies provided by the suppliers of new equipment attached to capital requests indicating promised improvements. But, these supplier-provided studies are usually unaccompanied by data offering proof of the promised improvements.

When considering changes to internal processes, the more enlightened companies collect data representing the performance of the process as it presently exists. Then, after the process change has been implemented, data is once again collected and compared to the data collected before the change was initiated. When a favorable comparison of the two data sets results, then, and only then, can success be declared.

Unfortunately, the comparison of the two data sets is too often based on the averages; the average of the data collected before the change and the average of the data collected after the change are compared, and a decision is made. To be more specific, making decisions based on averages alone, without taking into account the variation of the data that created the averages, can be misleading, expensive, and damaging.

For many years, I have used the following simple example to demonstrate this point: Consider that a nurse visited grade school A and weighed and recorded the average weight of forty of the fourth-grade children. The next day, the same nurse visited school B and weighed and recorded the average of forty of the fourth-grade children in that school. It is very likely the two averages would not be identical.

If the average weight of the children in school A was higher than the average weight of the children in school B, would it be logical to conclude the students in school A required more exercise during recess? Only the Exercise Equipment lobbyists in Congress would argue that point.

All data has variation, including the single data points we call averages. If the average weights of fourth-grade students in every school in the country were placed into a histogram, the variation of the averages would be normal and follow the familiar bell-shaped curve.

It is quite possible that, due to random chance, the average weight of the children in school A came from the high side of the distribution, and the average weight of the children in school B came from the low side of the distribution. If Congress authorized funds to upgrade the exercise equipment for grade schools, it would have done so as a result of being swindled by lobbyists and the normal variation of averaged data.

Expand this simple example to a manufacturing environment, and the reader may identify with past experiences, such as the following:

- The average tensile strength of the new, more expensive, material is higher than what we are presently using. It would be a benefit to change to the new supplier.
  - This decision might very well result in more expensive raw material that in fact does not have higher tensile strength. Both the average of the new raw material and the average of the existing new raw material might very well come from different areas of the same population of averages.
- Studies indicate we will average fewer problems with burrs once we install the modified tooling.
  - The decision to modify the tooling very likely will not reduce the burr problem because the variation of the burr problem is not changed by the modified tooling. The average scrap due to burrs is 5 percent, with a low experience of 0 percent and a high experience of 10 percent. The study was confounded by normal variation of percent defectives.

There is a simple tool provided by Microsoft Excel that will help guard against making erroneous decisions based on averaged data. In essence, this tool is termed analysis of variance (ANOVA); more specifically, it is in the Data Tool Pak and is termed ANOVA Single Factor. It is simple to use and will protect against the situations discussed in this section. See Chapter 8 for further discussion of ANOVA.

IN CONCLUSION

I would simply advise that a culture must be created that requires a manufacturer to recognize that variation exists in received raw material, and excessive variation in raw material results in excessive variation in the process to which it is introduced. Data must be received from suppliers indicating in numerical terms not only the averages of critical raw material characteristics but also the amount of variation either side of the average. A simple histogram is a good start.

8

Addendum

CONTROL CHARTS

The control chart concept enables us to predict long-term variation (the control chart limits) by means of analyzing short-term variation—the average range of data subgroups. The average chart represents the distribution of averaged data sequenced from the beginning to the end of a collection activity. In this example, four data points were recorded each hour because there were four terminals for each part. The average and range of each "subgroup" of four was calculated and used to create the average chart and range charts provided.

The average of the averages forms the centerline of the average chart. The upper and lower control limits, created using the average range of the subgroups, represent the calculated variation of the averages that can be expected over a period of time.

The arithmetic for calculating the Average and Range Control Chart limits is as follows:

X-Bar and R Chart Calculations

$\overline{X}$ (Average) = X total (sum of data points in subgroup) divided by number of data points in subgroup.

R (Range) = Largest measurement in subgroup minus smallest measurement in subgroup.

$\overline{\overline{X}}$ Grand Average = Summation of all averages divided by number of averages.

Upper and Lower Control Limits (UCL and LCL, respectively) for X-bar and R charts: The constants A_2, D_3, and D_4 are found in tables in any statistical process control text and depend on subgroup size.

UCL for $\overline{\overline{X}} = \overline{\overline{X}} + (A2 \times \overline{R})$
LCL for $\overline{\overline{X}} = \overline{\overline{X}} - (A2 \times \overline{R})$
UCL for $R = \overline{R} \times D_4$
LCL for $R = \overline{R} \times D_3$

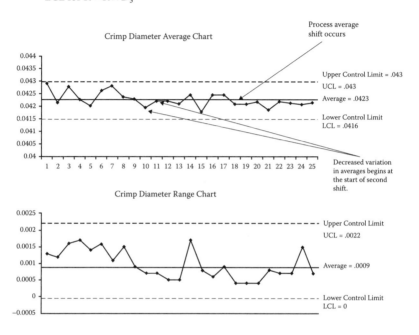

PROCESS CAPABILITY STUDIES

The process capability study is the only valid method of determining if a process is stable and capable. It is the very first step toward achieving process control as opposed to product control, and it is the only method of achieving a capability index (Cpk) of 1.33.

The Cpk concept is simple. The end user wants to have a reasonable expectation that all product received is within the stated specification. This expectation would necessitate the supplier to manufacture product so that there is leeway between the extreme ends of the normal variation of critical characteristics and the respective high and low specifications.

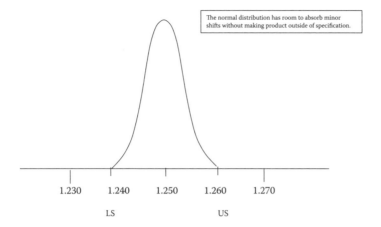

The industry standard for minimum Cpk is 1.33. A 1.33 Cpk means the center of the normal distribution curve is located at the customer nominal, and the total amount of variation is consuming no more than 75 percent of the total specification.

In the example, the total amount of specification is 1.270 – 1.240 = 0.030. The total amount of variation is 1.260 – 1.240 = 0.020. The Cpk is equal to total specification divided by total variation: 0.030/0.020 = 1.5.

If the center of the normal distribution is offset from nominal, it is necessary to determine a Cpl for the lower specification and a Cpu for the upper specification.

CPL = Product Average – Lower Specification ÷ ½ Total Variation

CPL = (0.260 – 0.255) ÷ ½ x (0.006)
CPL = 0.005 ÷ 0.003
CPL = 1.66

CPU = Upper Specification – Product Average ÷ ½ Total Variation

CPU = (0.285 – 0.260) ÷ ½ x (0.006)
CPU = 0.025 ÷ 0.003
CPU = 8.33

Both Cpl and Cpu must be above 1.33 for the process to be deemed capable. The lower of the two values is the reported Cpk. In this case, Cpk is 1.66.

STANDARD DEVIATION

There is an important convention concerning the manner in which a normal distribution is described. The center of any normal distribution is referred to as the average, and the width of the distribution is provided in terms of standard deviation or sigma. Outside the world of statisticians, the two terms *standard deviation* and *sigma* are used interchangeably. Every normal distribution has exactly three sigma (standard deviations) either side of the center (average).

This convention of describing a normal curve in terms of sigma makes for ease of communication when discussing data. If a supplier states that its process is centered at 0.500 with a sigma of 0.001, it is clear that the supplier can produce product between 0.497 and 0.503.

Process average = 0.500

One sigma = 0.001

Three sigma either side of the average

0.001 x 3 = 0.003

0.500 ± 0.003 = 0.497/0.503

EVOLUTIONARY OPTIMIZATION

The topic of design of experiments (DOE) and evolutionary optimization (EVOP) have been addressed in many texts, papers, and seminars. Whenever I engage in one of the many venues that present either topic, I think of Winston Churchill's description of the Soviet Union as "a mystery wrapped in an enigma."

The textbooks, papers, and seminars on either topic seem to make the concepts far more difficult than they are. It most often seems the material has been prepared in such a manner to be presented to people who already know the topics very well, people who are thoroughly familiar with formulas replete with Greek letters and other esoteric symbols.

Evolutionary optimization is a technique that enables a company with a great deal of shop floor discipline to improve on a process that is already stable and capable. Such improvements to a stable and capable process are in the true spirit of Continuous Improvement. Essentially, EVOP involves making minor changes to key process parameters previously identified by means of DOE. The minor changes are left in place, without adjustments, for a reasonably long period of time—several shifts or several days if applicable. During this time, numerous samples are collected and measured, and resulting data is analyzed to see if the minor process parameter changes reduced the variation of critical product characteristics. This procedure is repeated until the process parameters have been refined to a point at which variation of the product characteristics cannot be reduced any further.

Outside of a handful of companies, such as Toyota, this technique is not widely applied.

Of course, the EVOP technique involves adjusting more than one process parameter at a time.

There are many aspects of DOE and EVOP that I cannot cover in this text, but I would like to provide one of the simplest but very effective tools, which is a three-parameter, two-level matrix, presented in the table that follows. The pluses and minuses represent levels of a specific process parameter, chosen by the experimenter. The plus might represent high pressure.

Three-Factor, Two-Level Experimental Matrix

Run	Material Thickness	Air Pressure	Speed	Response
1	+	+	+	
2	+	+	−	
3	+	−	−	
4	+	−	+	
5	−	−	−	
6	−	−	+	
7	−	+	+	
8	−	+	−	

Glossary

Accuracy: Comparison to a known standard. A measurement device that measures a known standard without appreciable error is said to be *accurate*.

Assignable cause: An unusual occurrence that takes place within a process—unusual in that the variation resulting from an assignable cause is outside normal variation.

Average (X bar): The mean value of a subgroup. The average is calculated by adding the values within the subgroup and dividing by the number of values.

Brainstorming: An exercise in which a group of individuals expresses, and records, ideas concerning a specific problem. The essence of such an exercise lies in the openness and creativity of a free and unbiased exchange of ideas.

Capability: The ability of a process to produce all product well within customer specification. A process is said to be capable when it meets the minimum requirement of having the process average at nominal and taking up no more than a customer-specified amount of the specification.

Capability Index: The numerical value applied to the relationship between the total variation of a product characteristic and the customer specification. A capability index (Cpk) of 1.33 is the minimum requirement of many manufacturers.

Cause-and-effect exercise: A problem-solving tool used to identify the root cause of a problem. Fishbone diagrams and brainstorming are very effective means used to identify the root cause.

Control chart: A statistical process control tool that initially helps define the stability and capability of a process. The initial result of a process capability study is a *product* control chart that should evolve into a *process* control chart.

Control limits: Boundaries on control charts that identify the amount of normal variation we can expect from a product or process.

Cpk: *See* Capability index.

Discrimination: The ability of a measurement process to detect samples made during periods of normal variation.

Discrimination ratio: A numerical value approximately equal to the amount of product normal variation in terms of sigma divided by the amount of measurement process variation in terms of sigma. A discrimination ratio equal to or greater than 4.0 is required for a measurement process to be qualified for purposes of statistical analysis of a process output.

Histogram: A graphic tool that illustrates, in bar chart form, the distribution of data.

Individual control chart: A form of control chart that uses the range between individual data points to develop the control chart limits. An individual control chart is useful in the analysis of continuous processes such as extrusion and destruct measurement processes. The control chart limits of an individuals chart, unlike the control chart limits of the averages (X-bar) chart, also relate directly to the total amount of normal variation of the characteristic being studied.

Instability: The state that results in a process when assignable causes are present.

Lower control limit: The calculated lower boundary of a control chart representing the minus-three-sigma limit of the normal distribution.

Manufacturing process: Any combination of people, a measurement process, raw material, local environment, and standard procedures formed to complete an assigned task of manufacturing or service. Machining is a process, as is receiving and executing purchase orders.

Measurement process analysis (MPA): The statistical study of a measurement process to determine if it is precise and has an adequate *discrimination ratio*.

Nominal: The midpoint of a specification. In general, the nominal specification is the most desirable to achieve.

Normal curve: Sometimes called the bell curve because of its shape. The normal curve is characterized by having one peak and symmetrically trailing off to extreme ends on either side of the middle. A normal curve results when variable data is plotted from a process operating without any assignable causes present, only normal variation.

Normal variation: Variation due to natural and random occurrences. The differences of height among high-school seniors is a good example of normal variation.

Pareto chart: A tool that displays in bar chart form a frequency of occurrence within certain categories of interest. Usually, the highest category appears in the extreme left, and subsequent categories are presented in descending order. A Pareto chart separates the vital few categories from the trivial many.

Precision: The ability of a measurement process to record the same value within the bounds of normal variation when a measurement is repeated on the same sample, in the same location, by the same person, using the same measurement device.

Process average: The central tendency of a process. The process average is determined by collecting and converting data to a form such as a histogram or control chart.

Process capability study: The practice of analyzing product variation in order to determine if the process is stable and is capable of producing product that meets the customer's minimum Cpk requirement.

Process parameter: Usually a controllable factor related to one of the process elements, such as equipment line speed, raw material melt index, and so on.

Range: The difference between the largest and the smallest value with a group of variable data.

Sample: Statistical process control is based on the concept that the quality of an entire process can be confidently determined through the statistical evaluation of groups of random samples.

Sigma: *See* Standard deviation.

Stability: The ability of a process to produce consistent and predictable output. A stable process has only normal variation present; no assignable cause variation is present.

Standard deviation: A means of measuring the width of a distribution. A normal curve has three *standard deviations* either side of the process average. The term *sigma* is often used interchangeably with *standard deviation*.

Statistical process control (SPC): A term used to describe the tools and techniques that help to identify the sources of and reduce process variation.

SPC: *See* Statistical process control.

Statistical product control: A term used by the author to describe a misuse of statistical process control. When statistical process control charts are used to monitor product and make adjustments to the process to compensate for periods of process instability, statistical product control is being applied.

Tolerance: The amount of allowable variation about the nominal. Tolerances are often imposed without any quantitative knowledge of the capability of the process.

Upper control limit: The calculated upper boundary of a control chart representing the plus-three-sigma limit of the normal distribution.

Variation: Measurable deviation about a known point.

X-bar chart: The X-bar (averages) chart records the averages of groups of product selected over time. When the pattern of the averages is compared to certain criteria, a determination may be made regarding process stability. The control chart limits of the X-bar chart do not directly relate to the total amount of normal variation of the product characteristic being studied.

Bibliography

Grant, E. and Leavenworth, R. S. 1980. *Statistical Quality Control*. New York: McGraw-Hill, New York.

Relyea, D. B. 2011. *The Practical Application of the Process Capability Study*. New York: Taylor and Francis.

Ryan, T. P. 1989. *Statistical Methods for Quality Improvement*. New York: John Wiley & Sons.

Index

About the Author

Douglas B. Relyea is the founder and senior partner of Quality Principle Associates a New England-based consulting firm that specializes in the education and application of data analysis techniques to industrial problem solving.

Mr. Relyea has a degree in manufacturing engineering from Three Rivers Community College in Connecticut and a business degree from Eastern Connecticut State University.

He spent twenty years working at General Dynamics and a division of Rogers Corporation, specializing in extrusion, die stamping, machining and molding processes servicing the automotive and business equipment industries. During his time in industry he filled positions such as first-line supervisor, quality assurance manager, engineering manager, maintenance manager, and sales and marketing product manager. Most recently Mr. Relyea contributed Chapter 19 of the Wire Association International Wire Handbook. This chapter is entitled "Elements of Statistical Quality Control."

In 1987 he left industry and formed Quality Principle Associates.